MINDFULNESS

The Remarkable Truth
Behind Meditation and Being
Present in Your Life

OLIVIA TELFORD

MINDFULNESS: The Remarkable Truth Behind
Meditation and Being Present in Your Life
by Olivia Telford

© Copyright 2019 by Olivia Telford

All Rights Reserved.

No part of this publication may be reproduced, distributed, or transmitted in any form or by any means, including photocopying, recording, or other electronic or mechanical methods, without the prior written permission of the publisher, except in the case of brief quotations embodied in reviews and certain other noncommercial uses permitted by copyright law.

Disclaimer: This book is designed to provide accurate and authoritative information in regard to the subject matter covered. By its sale, neither the publisher nor the author is engaged in rendering psychological or other professional services. If expert assistance or counseling is needed, the services of a competent professional should be sought.

ISBN-10: 1077521553
ISBN-13: 978-1077521551

ALSO BY OLIVIA TELFORD

*Hygge: Discovering The Danish Art Of Happiness –
How To Live Cozily And Enjoy Life's Simple Pleasures*

*The Art of Minimalism: A Simple Guide to Declutter
and Organize Your Life*

Hygge and The Art of Minimalism: 2 in 1 Bundle

*Cognitive Behavioral Therapy: Simple Techniques to Instantly
Overcome Depression, Relieve Anxiety, and Rewire Your Brain*

CONTENTS

Introduction 7

Your Free Gift - 10 Minute Meditation 15

Chapter 1: What is Mindfulness? 21

Chapter 2: Simple Mindfulness Exercises 33

Chapter 3: How To Meditate 39

Chapter 4: Reducing Stress & Negativity With Mindfulness 45

Chapter 5: Mindfulness & Anger Management 62

Chapter 6: Depression & Mindfulness 71

Chapter 7: Mindfulness Exercises For Anxiety & Panic Attacks 84

Chapter 8: Building Better Habits With Mindfulness 93

Chapter 9: Beating Procrastination & Boosting Productivity With Mindfulness 103

Chapter 10: Beating "When...Then" Syndrome With Mindfulness 114

Chapter 11: Staying Present While Planning The Future .. 120

Chapter 12: Mindfulness & Relationships 127

Chapter 13: Making Mindfulness Part Of Everyday Life .. 135

Conclusion 144

INTRODUCTION

Imagine a treatment for anxiety, everyday stress, and depression that:

- Doesn't involve drugs
- Has no unpleasant side-effects
- Costs nothing
- Is available anywhere
- Can be used by anyone
- Has been scientifically proven to work

There really is a solution that ticks all these boxes. It's called "mindfulness." In this book, you're going to learn what mindfulness is, how to make it part of your everyday routine, and how it can transform your life.

You'll discover simple practices to help you feel better on every level – physically, psychologically, and spiritually. By the end of the book, you'll see the world, and yourself, in a whole new way. The future will feel less scary. The past will no longer cause you pain. You'll find it easier to forgive yourself and others, develop self-compassion, and find inner peace.

The only tools you need are an open mind and patience. You don't need to invest in special equipment, go on any retreats, or change your religious beliefs. You definitely don't need to become a Buddhist monk, renounce the modern world, or live a minimalist life.

At the same time, this book will challenge you to examine your values and lifestyle. For example, you'll be encouraged to ask yourself some tough questions about how you spend your time. The path ahead will be challenging, but it could be the most important journey of your life.

Perhaps you've tried therapy, self-help books, medication, and support groups. Maybe these measures helped for a while, but they didn't lead to real change. It's time to try a new approach.

Mindfulness is a way of life. It lets you befriend your authentic self, the real "you" hiding under years of social conditioning and unhealthy habits. When you accept yourself, you can take your life in a new direction. This sounds like a paradox, but by the time you finish this book, this simple idea will make perfect sense.

Are you ready? Turn the page to begin.

WHAT OTHERS ARE SAYING ABOUT *MINDFULNESS*

"Looking to rid stress and live more freely? In Mindfulness by Olivia Telford you will find comprehensive and straightforward techniques you can use today to instantly improve your well-being. After reading this book, I've never felt more empowered, happier and productive. Whether you've tried meditation before or are brand new to it, this is the perfect guide."

— Judy Dyer, author of Empath: A Complete Guide for Developing Your Gift and Finding Your Sense of Self

"An amazing little guide to the good life! Olivia Telford explains what mindfulness is, why it's so important, and how to cultivate it. Simple, actionable, and deeply insightful. I highly recommend this book!"

— Patrik Edblad, author of The Self-Discipline Blueprint: A Simple Guide to Beat Procrastination, Achieve Your Goals, and Get the Life You Want

"It's one thing to meditate, but it's a whole other thing to embody Presence throughout one's everyday life. While meditation can bring tremendous benefits, the real life-changing results come when you can infuse Presence into all aspects of your inner and outer life so that you live with true mindfulness. Olivia Telford has done the world a great service by writing a book that is packed with authentic exercises that allow you to become more mindful and present in many different aspects of your life. Whether you're new to meditative and mindfulness practices or have been practicing for years, this book can serve you in profound ways."

— Ziad Masri, author of Reality Unveiled: The Hidden Keys of Existence That Will Transform Your Life (and the World)

"A powerful, enlightening book that works its way into your heart and soul."

— Bella Jean, author of The Forever In Between: A Historical Western Romance Book

"A stellar job by Olivia Telford. Another one, really. I was never quite a 100% believer in the concept of mindfulness, but I get it now. I really do. For me, the best part really starts from Telford's telling of Buddhism and how that kickstarts and underlies the whole process. When you look at it that way, and through the lens of detachment from everything, then you can really start to make headway. It's a great read."

— Peter Hollins, author of The Science of Self-Learning: How to Teach Yourself Anything, Learn More in Less Time, and Direct Your Own Education

JOIN OUR MINDFULNESS GROUP

In order to maximize the value you receive from this book, I highly encourage you to join our tight-knit community on Facebook. Here you will be able to connect and share strategies with others practicing mindfulness and meditation in order to continue your growth.

Taking this journey alone is not recommended, and this can be an excellent support network for you.

It would be great to connect with you there,

Olivia Telford

To Join, Visit:
www.pristinepublish.com/mindfulgroup

DOWNLOAD THE AUDIO VERSION OF THIS BOOK FREE

If you love listening to audiobooks on-the-go or would enjoy a narration as you read along, I have great news for you. You can download the audio book version of Mindfulness for FREE (Regularly $14.95) just by signing up for a FREE 30-day audible trial!

Visit: www.pristinepublish.com/audiobooks

YOUR FREE GIFT - 10 MINUTE MEDITATION

I'm sorry to be the bearer of bad news, but life isn't about you! And the moment you accept this is when you will truly start living. We live in a world that justifies selfishness, and everything is about the self. The dominant thought process goes, "What am I going to get out of this? How is this situation going to benefit me? Who can I manipulate to give me what I want?" Society has trained us to believe that the more money we have, the more we can buy, and the happier we will be. But the evidence suggests that these things don't bring us fulfilment. Why? Because the ego is always going to want more. Some of the most successful people in the world are never satisfied. The private jet is never enough, multiple partners are never enough, a wardrobe full of designer clothes is never enough. The 25-room mansion, and properties all over the world are never enough. If the world has got it wrong, then what brings true contentment in life?

Knowing that your purpose on earth is to be a giver. We were created to be givers, to empty ourselves using our gifts and talents in order to make the world a better place. Our peace comes from living selflessly, and not selfishly. I believe that the root cause of the human condition is that we are not living the way we were created to live. We've been corrupted and it's causing us to malfunction. The physical manifestation of this is seen through anxiety, depression, stress, and the plethora of mental health issues that we suffer from. Have you noticed that the happiest people are those who have found their purpose, and that purpose is always connected to giving of themselves? That's because they are doing what they were created to do.

"This all sounds great," I hear you saying, "but what do I need to do to get to this point? How can I live a selfless life when I'm struggling with anxiety, overthinking, stress, and depression? I can barely make it through the day, let alone think about living for other people." May I submit to you that meditation is the key to freeing yourself from the mental prison you are currently locked in? Here's how.

Meditation helps you connect with your higher self. Right now, you are living far below your capabilities, but you are more powerful than you could ever imagine. Science proves that meditation rewires the brain. It strengthens certain areas in the brain and transforms your internal emotional state. It makes you more compassionate and improves your ability to focus. Why is that important? Because a wandering mind can't focus on the needs of others. Additionally, several studies have found that meditation is linked to compassionate behavior towards oneself and others. It basically makes us more altruistic, which is exactly what we need if we are going to live to our full potential.

Meditation will teach you how to disconnect from the world so you can connect with your inner world. How much time do you spend on social media connecting meaningfully with people you know? We know more about the lives of the latest celebrities than we do about ourselves. Some people have become so co-dependent that spending time alone scares them. Being continuously engaged has become the norm, and those who enjoy solitude are often ridiculed. But the irony is that solitude is the only way you can truly get to know yourself. Switching off the TV and putting down the phone to tune in to yourself is a terrifying prospect for some of us.

You're not alone. When I first started meditating, I was afraid of getting to know myself too. I was petrified of listening to the voices in my head because I'd spent most of my life running from them. The more I ran, the more I suffered, because I was running into the same like-minded people who didn't like themselves very much either. True love starts from within. If you don't love yourself, it's impossible to love anyone else. And how can you love yourself if you don't know yourself? It took me a while to get to know and love myself, and I'm still learning who I am. When I embraced solitude, and finally surrendered, I really started enjoying my own company. You've just got to take that leap of faith and do it because it works. I now have the peace and freedom I've always wanted. Meditation was a complete game changer for me; it even gave me the confidence to quit my job and start writing full time!

Unfortunately, meditation intimidates many people, and they have no idea how transformative it is. If you were to ask the average person what comes to mind when they think about meditation, they'll say something like, "A monk sitting on top of a hill thinking about nothing for hours." As you will discover, meditation is much more than the stereotypes portray. Furthermore, you can experience the full benefits by meditating for as little as ten minutes each day.

Do you want to enrich your life, free yourself from the burdens of anxiety, stress, and overthinking? Do you want to transcend the human mind and connect with the infinite source? Do you want to live an abundant life overflowing with peace, joy, and happiness? Do you want to find fulfilment in everything you do? Do you want to develop deeper relationships with your loved ones and improve your health? The information in this guide will help you achieve it. In this bonus e-book, you can expect to learn about the following:

- Exactly what meditation is and what it isn't
- The basics of meditation and the different types
- The health benefits of meditation
- Meditation techniques to help you overcome anxiety, stress, overthinking and insomnia

The aim of *10 Minute Meditation* is to take the fear out of meditation and make it accessible to all who desire to improve their lives on a deeper level. I truly believe that what you are about to read will radically transform your life.

Get *10 Minute Meditation* for Free by Visiting

www.pristinepublish.com/meditationbonus

CHAPTER 1:

WHAT IS MINDFULNESS?

"Mindfulness" has become a buzzword in personal development circles. You may have seen articles, magazines, and websites about it. Maybe you've seen ads for mindfulness classes, or you might have been offered mindfulness seminars at work.

MINDFULNESS IN A SINGLE SENTENCE

According to Mindful magazine, mindfulness can be summed up as:

> "…the basic human ability to be fully present, aware of where we are and what we're doing, and not overly reactive or overwhelmed by what's going on around us."[1]

Psychologist Shauna Shapiro, an internationally renowned mindfulness expert, explains that there are three key components to mindfulness:[2]

1. Intention, or "paying attention on purpose"
2. Attention
3. Attitude, specifically an attitude of non-judgmental acceptance

At first glance, the whole topic of mindfulness seems odd or redundant. After all, aren't we all aware of what we're doing?

Unfortunately, the answer is "No." Most of us go through life on autopilot. Our thoughts and emotions control us, not the other way around. Anxiety, stress, and depression are endemic in modern society. Too many of us feel out of control, scared, and overwhelmed. Mindfulness is about learning how to accept and work with your mind – and yourself. By extension, it's also about accepting your life and discovering the joy in ordinary, everyday moments.

Mindfulness Versus Mindlessness

You can think of mindfulness as the opposite of mindless action. When we behave mindlessly, we zone out. We stop experiencing our own lives. For example, have you ever sat down to eat a meal, only to get distracted by your phone, your own racing thoughts, or the view from your window?

If so, did you look down at your plate and realize that all the food was gone? Lots of us do this. Just think of how many meals the average person eats without even tasting them! Mindless eating isn't satisfying, and it can even make you gain weight. Later in the book, you'll learn how to gain control over mindless behaviors and unhelpful habits.

Mindfulness Exercise: An Introduction To Mindfulness

To appreciate what mindfulness means, you need to experience it for yourself. Try this exercise to help you gain insight into how it feels to live mindfully.

Step 1: Go outside and find a leaf. If you can't find one, a small pebble will also work.

Step 2: Set a timer for five minutes.

Step 3: Look at the leaf as though you've never seen a leaf before. Turn it over slowly. Take in its color, shape, weight, and texture. Put it up to the light. How does the color change? If your mind starts to wander, bring your attention back to the leaf.

This simple practice shows you what mindfulness is all about. By focusing all your attention on a single object, you have no choice but to live in the present.

Mindfulness Exercise: Tracking Your Wandering Mind

Keep a pen and paper with you throughout the day. Every time you catch your mind wandering away from your current task, make a mark on the piece of paper. It should only take you a few hours to see why mindfulness will benefit you.

Where Did Mindfulness Come From?

Modern mindfulness practices have ancient roots. In Buddhism, it's at the heart of spiritual practice. To understand the link between Buddhism and mindfulness today, it's helpful to understand what Buddhism teaches about the mind.

The Buddha taught his followers that most human suffering is self-generated. Although external events can cause us pain, it's how we think about and respond to these events that matters most.

He also believed that humans make themselves unhappy by grasping after things they don't already have, such as relationships and material possessions. As long as we have these "cravings," we will never be satisfied. The key to inner peace is to understand, and then detach ourselves from, these cravings.

Common cravings include the desire for money, status, and beauty. There is nothing intrinsically wrong with wanting these things, but when we start making them the central focus of our lives, we're in trouble. For example, aiming for a promotion is all well and good, but working so hard that you lose sight of your values and alienate your family is not.

So, how can we learn to identify and overcome these cravings? Buddhists turn to meditation, among other methods, to help them become aware of their cravings. Gaining insight into the workings of one's own mind is a key step to overcoming suffering.

The Difference Between Mindfulness & Meditation

"Mindfulness" and "meditation" are often used interchangeably, but it's important to be clear on the differences.

Meditation is normally a formal, seated practice. There are several types, including mantra-based meditation, guided meditation, and loving-kindness meditation. We'll take a closer look at these practices in later chapters.

You have to make time for a meditation session. Meditators usually start a session with a goal in mind, such as sending love to someone else. They normally begin with breathing exercises that allow them to focus on inhalation and exhalation. The meditator then "turns inward," focusing on an idea, word, or external object such as a candle flame.

Mindfulness can take the form of meditation, but it goes beyond formal practice. You can be mindful anywhere. There's no need to sit down and contemplate a single idea or object. In summary, you don't have to practice meditation to be mindful. However, formal meditation is well worth a go, because scientific research has demonstrated the positive effects it has on the mind and body.

Mindfulness doesn't solve your problems. Instead, it provides you with a space to simply sit with them, and accept your situation for what it is. Buddhists refer to mindfulness practices as sati.[3] In this book, you'll learn how to integrate mindfulness into your everyday life.

The Satipatthana Sutta

Known as the "Discourse on the Foundations of Mindfulness," the Satipatthana Sutta is generally considered the most important Buddhist text on mindfulness meditation. The text outlines Buddha's teachings on mindfulness, framing it as an essential faculty anyone can develop.

According to the Sutta, mindfulness has to be deliberately cultivated. Buddha acknowledged that practicing it isn't easy. Satipatthana meditation encourages personal insight but also improves general concentration. In this context, "insight" means a keen awareness of seeing reality, perhaps for the first time.[4]

The Buddha frequently referred to the Four Foundations of Mindfulness:[5]

1. Body: When you are mindful, you notice how it feels to live in your body. You notice your breathing patterns, posture, and any aches, pains, or itching. The Buddha taught his followers to think of their bodies, not as a possession, but merely a home or vehicle they happen to be inhabiting. Breathing exercises are an effective means of getting in touch with the body. We'll come back to the breath many times in this book.

2. Feelings: Mindful people are willing to face their feelings, knowing that all emotions are transient. They are prepared to label feelings as they arise, watching them come and go. Mindfulness teaches

us that our feelings don't have to define us as individuals.

3. Consciousness: Mindful people acknowledge not only their emotions but their general state of mind. For instance, during a mindfulness session, you may acknowledge that you are "tired" or "content."

4. Dharma: This Sanskrit word is hard to define in English. Roughly translated, it means "the nature of things" or "law of nature." It can refer to Buddhist teaching, but it can also be used to describe the world around us. Everyone carries their own history and set of experiences, so Buddhists say that everyone's dharma is different. Someone in tune with their personal dharma is following their unique path, or calling.

This book isn't an in-depth discussion of Buddhist philosophy, but it's helpful to understand the roots of contemporary mindfulness. If you'd like to learn more about Buddhist teachings, The Buddhist Society (thebuddhistsociety.org) is a good place to start.

How Buddhist Ideas Entered Western Medicine

In the 1970s, biologist Professor Jon Kabat-Zinn pioneered a new approach for people living with chronic illness. Over an eight-week period, he trialed a stress-reduction program based on mindfulness practices. The course, which is offered at the Center for Mindfulness at UMASS Medical School, teaches people how to use mindful activity to cope with day-to-day stress and chronic pain.[6]

Although he was heavily influenced by Buddhist teachings as a student, Kabat-Zinn teaches mindfulness from a secular perspective. Mindfulness researchers aren't usually very interested in learning complex Buddhist philosophy. Instead, they concentrate on teaching and implementing exercises that improve a person's mental and physical health.

Kabat-Zinn's approach is now known as Mindfulness-Based Stress Reduction, or MBSR. We'll take a closer look at the principles underlying MBSR later in the book. Since those early days, mindfulness has become a popular tool for therapists, trainers, educators, and coaches. Hundreds of peer-reviewed studies have shown it to be effective for people with anxiety, depression, stress, eating disorders, and other forms of emotional distress. MBSR is still taught today, at dozens of centers across the US.

Why Do We Need Mindfulness?

In the Western world, stress and mental illness are at an all-time high. One possible cause is our hectic lifestyles. Most of us have to balance a job and a family, and we are working long hours just to make ends meet. There are also many global problems to worry about. Thanks to the internet, it's easier than ever to read about the financial insecurity, climate change, and political turmoil that threaten us.

We also have to contend with social media. Scrolling through profiles and feeds that show other people enjoying themselves can be disheartening, and encourage us to make unhelpful comparisons. If we don't measure up to our peers, or to society's standards, we feel inferior and depressed.

In summary, we have plenty to worry about in the 21st century. We need psychological defenses against the stressors in our lives.

If we are to solve society's problems, we need to work together. For that to happen, we need to value others and take the time to see their point of view. Mindfulness can help us adopt a compassionate attitude and increase our empathy.

For example, a study published in *Psychological Science* showed that people who went on an eight-week meditation course were three times more likely to help out a stranger in need than those in the control condition.[7] If enough of us learn to be mindful of others and tune into their suffering, society could change in a profound way.

What Does The Research Say?

Mindfulness isn't just appealing on a common-sense level. It's also backed up by rigorous scientific research.

Here are a few key findings from the last two decades of research:

1. **Mindfulness makes you more resilient in the face of stress**
   Mindfulness practices can't make life's problems disappear. However, they can help stabilize you during life's more trying moments. Research with

students shows that learning and practicing mindfulness skills significantly lowers stress and risk of burnout.[8]

2. **Mindfulness can improve your relationships**
Married couples who score higher on measures of mindfulness are happier.[9] This makes sense; if you are mindful in your relationships, you'll be better at staying calm when things get tough. You'll also be better at understanding and communicating your own emotions without resorting to angry or impatient outbursts. In the long run, this could have huge implications. How many divorces could be prevented if couples learned how to approach their differences in a mindful way?

3. **Mindfulness can enhance your working memory**
One of the most exciting benefits of mindfulness is the effect it has on cognitive functioning. The term "cognitive functioning" refers to the day-to-day mental tasks we all have to do. Someone with good cognitive functioning can plan tasks, stay focused, and commit new information to memory.

In one study, participants were split into two groups. One group was given four meditation training sessions, and the other was invited to listen to an audiobook instead. The people in the meditation session enjoyed a significant drop in fatigue and anxiety and achieved higher scores on memory tests.[10]

If you often forget things, you might assume you are just cursed with a poor memory. However, mindlessness is more likely to be the real cause of your woes. To remember something, you need to take in new information. Otherwise, you won't be able to recall it later. By learning how to be mindful of your surroundings, you'll feel less flustered and forgetful.

4. **Mindfulness can improve your physical health**
Although more research is needed, there's plenty of evidence to suggest that mindfulness can improve your physical health. For example, psychologists have discovered that mindfulness can strengthen your immune system and reduce chronic inflammation. It's still early, but some researchers have speculated that regular mindfulness practices could even slow down the aging process.[11]

5. **Mindfulness can help you make better choices**
Our lives are defined by our decisions. Unfortunately, it's all too easy to make hasty choices that don't benefit us or other people. Mindfulness practices teach you how to make sound decisions based on the facts in front of you, rather than your emotions or irrational fears.

Note that being mindful isn't about pushing your emotions to one side and acting like a robot. It's about understanding how to tame them when they work against you. Staying mindful lets you avoid making poor decisions that come back to haunt you later.

You've Nothing To Lose & Everything To Gain

In summary, mindfulness offers a lot of benefits – all for a minimal time investment. No matter how busy you are, mindfulness can become part of your daily routine. Most of the exercises in this book take 10 minutes or less. You can extend your sessions if you like, but you only need a short period of time to feel the difference.

Summary

- Mindfulness is the act of paying attention.
- Mindfulness is not the same thing as meditation. Although meditation is a useful way to practice mindfulness, it is only one path.
- Mindfulness is rooted in Buddhism, but you don't need to change your religious beliefs to use mindfulness.
- Mindfulness offers lots of physical and psychological benefits, including reduced stress and a more effective immune system.

CHAPTER 2:

SIMPLE MINDFULNESS EXERCISES

In the last chapter, you got a brief taste of mindfulness. In this chapter, you'll learn several more exercises that will help you lead a more mindful life.

Later in this book, you'll discover how mindfulness can help you overcome specific problems, such as depression and anxiety. We'll also talk about how it can be used as an anti-procrastination and goal-setting tool.

First, we're going to cover three practices that take less than five minutes. These are general exercises that you can use any time. Think of them as multipurpose tools; whatever your specific problem or situation, they will equip you with the basic skills you need to start your journey to mindfulness.

The more you use these tools, the better. Try each one several times. If you like it, continue; if not, experiment with another.

THREE SIMPLE MINDFULNESS PRACTICES

Simple Mindfulness Practice #1: Mindful Breathing

Watching your breath is the simplest practice of all. The aim is to breathe as usual while attending to the sensations in your body.

1. Sit or lie down. If you are feeling tired, it may be best to sit up so you don't fall asleep.
2. Close your eyes if you prefer.
3. Pay attention to your breathing. Observe how it feels to inhale and exhale air.
4. If your thoughts start wandering off, bring your focus back to your breath.

Simple Mindfulness Practice #2: Tasting Food

We take the act of eating for granted, but when was the last time you slowed down and really appreciated a meal or snack? This practice uses food as a focal point of awareness.

Follow these steps:[12]

1. Choose a small piece of food, such as a raisin or a nut.
2. Look at the food carefully. Notice what it looks like, how it feels in your hands, and how it smells.
3. Put the food in your mouth. Notice how it tastes. Move it around your mouth for a couple of minutes. Finally, chew it carefully and swallow.
4. Pay attention to the sensation of the food moving down your throat and into your stomach.

You'll probably notice various thoughts popping into your head. For example, you might think, "I don't like raisins" or "This is dumb, what's the point?"

That's OK. You don't have to empty your head of all thoughts. Your mission is to keep your attention on the present moment as much as possible. If your mind wanders off, just bring it back to the task at hand.

Simple Mindfulness Practice #3: Listening To Music

Any kind of music can be a meditation tool, but choosing a soothing track will make the experience more relaxing.

1. Sit or lie down in a comfortable position.
2. Play the music.
3. Follow each note. Pay attention to the pitch and tempo. If your mind conjures up images or memories, observe them. Don't wish them away. Just notice how your brain and body respond to the sounds.
4. As the track comes to an end, pay attention to how your body feels. Does it feel lighter? Softer? Heavier? Just notice.
5. Pay attention to your mood. Do you feel calmer? Unmoved? Uncomfortable? Whatever you feel is perfectly normal. There is no "correct" response here. The aim is to practice noticing what is going on in your mind and body.

If you use public transport, why not try this exercise on your journey to work? It will put you in a calm frame of mind that will help you face the day ahead. You can also use it on the way home to decompress after a stressful day in the office.

LONGER PRACTICES

If you have more than five minutes to spare, try a body scan or a mindful walk. Once or twice a week is enough, especially when you're first starting out. Take it easy. Do what fits into your lifestyle.

Mindfulness Exercise: Body Scanning

Body scanning makes for a wonderfully relaxing start or end to your day:[13]

1. Set aside at least half an hour, but an hour is best. Give yourself the chance to feel the benefits of this exercise.
2. Lie down on a comfortable surface. You may wish to place a small cushion or folded blanket beneath your head. Turn off any bright lights.
3. Close your eyes.
4. Notice your breath. Notice how it feels to breathe in and out. If your mind drifts away, bring your attention back to the flow of air in and out of your body.
5. Inhale and switch your attention to any part of your body. Follow your intuition.

6. Notice any sensations that arise. You may notice tingling, warmth, numbness, aching, lightness, fullness – or a combination of the above. Some people prefer to begin at the head and move downward, while others start with their feet. Take an attitude of curiosity rather than judgment.
7. When you have finished scanning your body, focus on your breathing again. When you're ready, open your eyes and sit up.

Mindfulness Exercise: Mindful Walking

Research has shown that walking in a green space, such as a park, improves your mood and sharpens your concentration. You'll also benefit from moving your body because exercise helps you sleep better. If you spend a lot of time sitting down during the day, walking may be more appealing than seated practices.

Here's how to take a mindful walk:[14]

1. Before you begin walking, tune into your body. Notice your posture and temperature. Feel the sensation of your feet on the ground. How do they feel inside your shoes?
2. Start walking. Move slightly slower than usual.
3. As you walk, notice how your heels, then your toes make contact with the ground.
4. Take deep breaths, noticing how it feels to breathe in and out.
5. Keep your gaze soft.

6. When emotions and thoughts pop up, acknowledge them without judgment or condemnation.
7. Walk in this way for as long as you like.
8. End your practice slowly. Give yourself a few seconds to feel the earth beneath your feet.

Any of the exercises in this chapter will help you feel less stressed. They are all perfect for taking a bit of time out of a busy day.

Summary

- The three simplest mindfulness exercises involve focusing on your breath, tasting some food, and listening to a piece of music.
- Body scanning is a longer practice but is well worth trying if you have the time.
- Mindful walking is a great alternative if you feel too restless to sit still or lie down.
- You don't have to use all the practices in this chapter. Using one or two a few times per week is enough to trigger real change.

CHAPTER 3:

HOW TO MEDITATE

You don't have to start meditating to lead a mindful life, but give it a try – you'll be glad you did! Meditation reduces stress, helps reduce anxiety, enhances your attention span, improves your memory, lowers your blood pressure, and promotes better sleep.[15]

In this chapter, you'll experiment with three types of meditation. We're going to look at mantra meditation, loving-kindness meditation, and guided meditation.

MEDITATING FOR THE FIRST TIME

Keep your expectations realistic, otherwise you may become discouraged and give up. Not many people can sit down and meditate for an hour on their first attempt. (Not that you need to meditate for this long anyway!) It takes time to cultivate your attention span, so aim to meditate for five minutes at first. Twenty or thirty minutes per day is ideal, but a few times per week is much better than nothing.

Be prepared to experience a range of emotions. You may feel self-conscious, anxious, or frustrated. This is completely normal! Sit with these feelings. Notice them come and go. Gently bring your attention back to your breath, mantra, or other primary focus of your practice.

Mantra Meditation

"Mantra" is a Sanskrit term derived from two roots, "man" and "trai." "Man" translates as "to think" or "mind," and "trai" means "tool," "protect," or "free from." Therefore, a mantra is a tool used to liberate the mind.[16]

Mantra meditation involves focusing on, and repeating, a mantra. Mantras are not usually spoken aloud but repeated internally by your inner voice. A mantra provides a point of fixation for your mind during meditation. It's hard to focus on two or more thoughts at once. By using a mantra, you cut through mental chatter and stay in the present moment.

Here's how to get started:[17]

1. Pick a mantra. Mantras should be short, positive, and easy to repeat. Some people prefer traditional mantras such as "Om" or "Sat, Chit, Ananda." Using a mantra in a language you don't understand can help you concentrate, because it is less likely to trigger your emotions than English words or phrases.

   However, you may find that an English mantra holds more appeal. Experiment with both to find what works for you. Popular mantras include "I am enough," "I change my thoughts, I change my world," and "I love you, I am sorry, please forgive me, thank you."

2. Sit down in a quiet place, free from distractions.
3. Close your eyes. You can meditate with your eyes open, but most people find that closing their eyes helps them focus their attention.
4. Set your intention. Decide why you are meditating right here, right now. For example, do you want to calm yourself down? Or perhaps you want to feel a sense of kinship with those around you?
5. Ground yourself with some deep breathing. Spend a couple of minutes watching your breath. Inhale and exhale, feeling air fill and leave your lungs.
6. Begin repeating your mantra. Keep a steady rhythm. If it feels right, you can chant it aloud.
7. When your mind wanders, pull your focus back to the mantra. At first, you'll have to do this every few seconds.
8. Repeat your mantra for as long as you like.

Loving-Kindness Meditation

Loving-kindness meditation, also known as "metta meditation," helps you foster goodwill towards yourself and others. Here's how to do it:[18]

1. With your eyes closed, sit in a comfortable position.
2. Take a few deep breaths.
3. Begin by receiving love from others. Imagine that someone who has shown you kindness, such as a family member or teacher, is standing to your right. Feel the love emanating from them. Now, imagine

another person you love and admire standing to your left. Again, feel their love and compassion. Alternatively, you can imagine that the same person is standing on both your left and right sides.
4. Now picture yourself surrounded by everyone who cares for you. Welcome their love and care. Let yourself feel warm, safe, and protected.
5. Think about the person standing to your right. Send them love. Say to them, "May you live with ease, may you be happy, may you be free from pain."
6. Repeat #5, but this time, direct your love to the person on your left.
7. Next, think of a neutral person in your life. This should be someone you neither like nor dislike, such as the person who sometimes serves you at the grocery store. Say to them, "Just as I wish to, may you also live with ease and happiness."
8. Repeat #7, but this time, send your good wishes out to the world as a whole. It may help to picture the earth as a globe. You could picture it from space, or as a small ball directly in front of you.

Some people also send love and warm wishes to people they actively dislike. This can be healing, but may also stir up some difficult emotions. Start with the practice above, and then extend it to those who have harmed you if it feels safe to do so.

Guided Meditation

As the name implies, guided meditation involves following instructions from someone else. By following their voice, you enter a state of consciousness that helps you relax, accept your negative thoughts, and cope with challenging emotions.

Some guided meditations ask you to focus on your breathing or a mantra. Others are more elaborate, involving lengthy visualizations. For example, your guide may help you enter a mental "safe space" that feels peaceful and serene.

If you want to try guided meditation, you have several options. You can attend a class run by a meditation teacher, or you can buy recordings or CDs you can listen to in the privacy of your own home. There are plenty of free guided meditations online. Here are two sites to get you started:

- https://www.tarabrach.com/guided-meditations/
- https://chopra.com/articles/guided-meditations

You can also write your own guided meditation scripts, record them, and then play them back as you meditate. Hearing your own voice can be strange at first, but after a few sessions, it will feel natural to listen to yourself. Follow a few pre-recorded guided meditations first for inspiration.

Respect Your Meditation Time

Create a peaceful meditation area in your home. A spare room is ideal, but a corner of your bedroom or living room will work just as well. Make it special. You could buy a new cushion, place some candles in your space, or hang a quote or picture that inspires you. When the weather permits, pick a quiet corner in your garden.

If you live with other people, you may need to get up slightly earlier or go to bed later than usual to carve out some time for yourself, especially if you are a parent. At first, you might feel more tired during the day. Stick with it! Research shows that meditation actually raises your energy levels, meaning you won't miss those 30 minutes of sleep.[19]

Summary

- You don't have to learn to meditate to lead a mindful life, but lots of people find it helpful.
- Mantra meditation involves focusing on a word or phrase.
- Loving-kindness meditation is a wonderful, healing way to send love and warmth to yourself and others. It can help you release grudges or attachments to the past.
- Guided meditations are useful if you want some support. You can attend a class, download meditations, or create your own.

CHAPTER 4:

REDUCING STRESS & NEGATIVITY WITH MINDFULNESS

We all have to deal with stress. Even if you aren't in a high-powered job, live alone, and have few obligations, you still come up against situations that make you feel overwhelmed. In this chapter, we'll look at how mindfulness can reduce your stress levels and help you become a more positive person.

First, a note of caution. You can't lead a stress-free life. Stress is part of the human experience. It's the price we pay for setting goals, living in the real world, and setting high standards for ourselves. A modest amount of stress is actually good for you. For instance, stress can give you the edge at work, giving you the buzz you need to get a project done.

When Stress Becomes Harmful

Although some stress is beneficial, prolonged stress has a devastating effect on our minds and bodies. When you feel stressed, your body releases a hormone called cortisol. Cortisol is useful during emergency situations because it raises our blood sugar and gives our muscles easier access to energy reserves.

However, research has shown a link between elevated cortisol and serious diseases such as type 2 diabetes. Scientists have also discovered that heightened cortisol levels may be associated with obesity. Cortisol can encourage your body to store excess fat around your abdomen. This pattern of fat distribution increases your risk of diabetes and heart disease.[20]

So, can mindfulness help get your cortisol levels under control? Absolutely! A study published in the journal *Neuropsychobiology* showed that cortisol levels drop significantly after just 8 weeks of mindfulness training. The researchers also measured cortisol levels in long-term meditators and found that the longer they had been practicing meditation, the less cortisol there was in their blood.[21]

MINDFULNESS & LETTING GO

Many of us are addicted to the idea of being in control. We like to think that we can control our relationships, our children, our careers, our finances, and so on. To some extent, this is correct. The way you conduct yourself at work, for example, can make the difference when it comes to getting a promotion.

Unfortunately, the reality is that many events are beyond our control. When something happens that makes us realize this uncomfortable truth, we get upset and stressed. To continue the example above, you can choose how much effort you put into your job, but if the board of directors decides that they need to lay off dozens of people, there's not much you can do about it. In times like these, you need to anticipate, accept, and cope with stress instead of lamenting the unfairness of life.

The prospect of accepting reality for what it is, not what we want it to be, can be terrifying. Buddhists are keenly aware of this. They believe that our addiction to control is an unhealthy attachment that only results in suffering.

Paradoxically, the better you are at accepting your distress and anxiety in any given situation, the happier you will become. When you develop self-compassion and self-acceptance, your stress will pass quicker, leaving you with time and energy to plan your next move.

Mindfulness Isn't The Same As Apathy

You might assume that if you give up fighting for control, you'll give up on life altogether. Society teaches us that those who set inflexible goals and push themselves to succeed are to be praised and admired, so it's hardly surprising that any notion of accepting the natural ups and downs of life seems suspicious.

The key to leading a more relaxed life is to accept that the only thing you can really control in life is your response to it. As you practice mindfulness, you'll come to appreciate that this is an empowering position.

After all, if you can't control the world around you, you are free to focus on how you react. This doesn't mean you can't make plans for your future or set goals, merely that you realize everything is impermanent. Few things work out exactly as we hope.

Noticing Stress In Your Body

Having accepted that stress is normal and inevitable, the next step is to train yourself how to pick up on your early warning signs. Mindfulness is a great stress detector!

Some of us are so out of touch with our own bodies that we don't even realize when they are starting to show the signs of strain.

Here are some clues that your stress levels are rising:

- Your head feels foggy, you're tired, and you find it hard to concentrate.
- Your appetite changes; some people eat more under stress, whereas others can't face food.
- Your muscles feel tense.
- You feel as though you could cry at any moment.
- You have a headache or migraine.
- You experience palpitations.
- You seem to be sweating more than usual.
- Your skin feels itchy; if you suffer from eczema, it may feel more irritated than usual.

Use the basic mindfulness exercises in Chapter Two to check in with yourself throughout the day. You may be surprised to learn that you are considerably more stressed than you imagined. That's normal! The busier and more stressed you are, the less likely you are to slow down for a few minutes and think about what's actually going on in your body.

How To Handle The Signs Of Stress

Often, merely tuning into your body and sitting with your feelings is enough to lower your stress levels. Accepting what is happening around you and within you fosters acceptance, and it gives you the chance to learn that all emotions pass.

The following exercise will help you cope with short-term stress.

Mindfulness Exercise: Riding The Wave Of Stress

The next time you start feeling annoyed or agitated, try this quick exercise that allows you to ride out stress instead of fighting it:[22]

1. Wherever you are, stand or sit still.
2. Take a deep breath, then briefly scan your body from your head to your feet.
3. Watch for signs of stress. Are your hands curling into fists? Are you sweating? Are your shoulders tense?
4. Imagine that your stress is like a large wave, crashing towards you.
5. As the wave reaches its peak, picture yourself literally riding or surfing it. Picture yourself sitting or standing on the peak, confident yet serene.
6. Let yourself feel content and proud for negotiating the wave, whilst remembering that you will need to keep doing this throughout your life.

MINDFULNESS, LONG-TERM STRESS, & BURNOUT

So far, we've talked about short-term stress — those everyday moments that make you feel overwhelmed. But what about stress that accumulates over time? The kind of stress that leaves you feeling burned out and depleted?

Burnout can happen to anyone, including stay-at-home parents and students. It's a state of complete physical and emotional exhaustion triggered by a slow build-up of stress, usually over many months. Burnout is a serious health issue, and it can take a long time to recover from the aftereffects.

Here are the most common signs:

- Feeling as though every day is a "bad day."
- No longer finding any sense of purpose or enjoyment in your life or work.
- Feeling taken for granted and underappreciated by everyone around you.
- Feeling tired and drained every day.
- Feeling as though all your tasks are dull, mind-numbing, or repetitive.
- Other physical symptoms include frequent minor illnesses, aches and pains, and changes to your sleep or eating patterns.

Stress is a sign that you care too much about your situation. It's the result of expending too much effort trying to change it. On the other hand, if you are burned out, you start checking out. Nothing seems to matter anymore. You may use drugs, alcohol, or other destructive behaviors to cope. In severe cases, a person with burnout may conclude that life is no longer worth living.

Some people are more prone than others to burnout. Personality is a major factor. If you are a perfectionist with an all-or-nothing thinking style and a love of control, you are at heightened risk. Perfectionists can always find areas for improvement. They find it hard to stop, slow down, and acknowledge their own achievements.

So, how can mindfulness prevent burnout? As you may have guessed, mindfulness helps you let go of things you can't control, which short-circuits stress. Mindfulness also helps you appreciate what is going well, and it gives you breathing space when you find yourself worrying about the future. Finally, living in the present alerts you to the first signs of burnout. The earlier you seek help, the better.

Research shows that mindfulness practice can lower the risk of burnout in high-stress professions. For instance, a review in the *American Journal of Occupational Therapy* concludes that "there is strong evidence for the use of mindfulness practice to reduce job burnout among health care professionals and teachers."[23] If mindfulness works for people in stressful occupations, it probably works for those working in less pressured environments too.

MINDFULNESS & NEGATIVITY

By definition, no one enjoys negative feelings, but they are a fact of life. Even if you have a wonderful job, plenty of money, a loving partner, and lots of friends, there will still be times when life beats you down. Learning to work with your negative emotions will help you weather the storms of life.

Human beings tend to focus on negative, rather than positive events. This is known as the "negativity bias." We all know that it's easier to dwell on the bad things that happen to us during the day, instead of appreciating the highlights.

From an evolutionary perspective, there's a good reason for the negativity bias. Our ancestors needed to remain alert to threats around them. This tendency is great for our survival as a species, but it can make us miserable if we pay too much attention to everything that upsets us.

The human brain is sophisticated, but it reacts to modern inconveniences, such as waiting in a long queue, as though they represent a threat to our lives. In becoming mindful, we learn to accept sadness, fear, and anger so that they no longer have the power to spoil our day.

Mindfulness Helps You Accept Negative Emotions

Most people make the mistake of trying to argue themselves out of their negative emotions. They tell themselves things like:

"Other people have it worse."

"Just pull yourself together."

"Just distract yourself; it's not that hard to forget about it."

Unfortunately, these strategies don't work in the long-term. They might work to temporarily stuff down the pain, but they are all forms of avoidance. Avoiding feelings only creates further tension and fear, which results in more negativity.

As spiritual teacher and writer Eckhart Tolle notes, "What you resist, persists." If you want to recover from your scariest feelings, you must embrace them.

Mindfulness Exercise: Working With Negative Emotions

Mindfulness expert Melli O'Brien, also known as "Mrs. Mindfulness," offers this six-step practice you can use when you feel swamped by negative emotions:[24]

1. As soon as you realize that you're feeling a negative emotion, take a moment to pause. Take a few deep breaths.
2. Let yourself acknowledge that you are experiencing the emotion. Say, "There is [emotion] in me" or "I feel [emotion]."
3. Hold the emotion. Accept that it's there. Don't fight it. Your mind may conjure up a mental image, perhaps of the situation that triggered the emotion. Whatever comes up, sit with it. After a couple of minutes, you'll realize that even the strongest emotion doesn't define you.
4. Watch the emotion ebb and flow, like a wave crashing against a shore. Remember that no feeling lasts forever.

5. Once you have made peace with your emotion and accepted its existence, you can undertake some gentle investigation. Your task here isn't to berate yourself, merely to understand what triggered it. Ask yourself:

> "What was I thinking about before this emotion came along?"
>
> "What was I doing?"
>
> "Have I made any judgments about myself or others that prompted these feelings?"
>
> "Beyond accepting my feelings, do I actually need to do anything about this situation?"

This exercise gives you breathing room. It lets you step back from your emotions and realize that they don't have to suck you in. Negative people tend to take their own thoughts very seriously. When you overcome this tendency, you'll find that life begins to feel much lighter. It's not that we should – or can – get rid of all negative thoughts, just that we need to learn to sit with them if we want to enjoy better psychological health.

Mindfulness Exercise: Name It, Tame It

This practice puts some distance between you and your emotions. It's simple and quick and can have profound results.[25]

1. When you feel a negative emotion swirling inside of you, stop and pause. Take a few deep breaths.

2. As you feel each emotion, label it, speaking aloud. For example, "Sad, angry, frustrated."
3. As you label each feeling, acknowledge it. Give it space. Let yourself feel detached from it. You may need to label the feeling several times, taking deep breaths in between each repetition.

Remember, all feelings will pass eventually, whatever you do.

The Dangers Of Emotional Contagion

Do you know someone who makes your heart sink whenever they enter the room? Do you have a friend or relative who always leaves you feeling negative, dissatisfied, or even depressed after just a few minutes in their company?

This phenomenon is called "emotional contagion." Along with our own emotional responses to the things that happen in our lives, we also have to learn how to handle other peoples' feelings. Otherwise, we can find ourselves at the mercy of their moods. If you work with a negative person, your emotional wellbeing will suffer unless you shield yourself from their feelings.

Mindfulness helps us respond to people around us in a sensitive and caring way, without getting caught up in their emotions. The first step is to work out who in your life is bringing you down.

Mindfulness Exercise: How Does This Person Make You Feel?

The next time you meet up with someone, whether it's a friend, relative, or coworker, check in with your body before and after your time together. Compare how you were feeling before your conversation and how you feel after spending time together.

Does your body feel more or less tense? Is your breathing slower or faster? Are your thoughts mostly positive or negative? Do you feel more or less enthusiastic about life in general?

Repeat this exercise, with different people, several times over the course of a few weeks. You'll start to notice that some people leave you feeling energized and positive, whereas others drain your spirit. You don't need to do anything with this information yet; just adopt the role of observer.

How To Respond To Other Peoples' Negativity

Staying mindful when you're dealing with someone else takes practice, but it can be done. Try to stop taking everything personally. Realize that, for the most part, someone else's bad mood has nothing to do with you.

Psychologist David J. Pollay calls this the "Law of the Garbage Truck." He points out that most people carry around a host of problems and bring their negative attitude wherever they go. If you aren't careful, they will happily dump it on you or anyone else who comes along.[26]

The next time someone starts trying to offload their negativity onto you, smile and deflect the conversation elsewhere. Remind yourself that you don't have to accept their garbage.

At the same time, remember that you never know the full story. It's possible that one of their relatives is sick or that they are facing major stress at work. Try to give them the benefit of the doubt.

You can also create a "pause policy." If someone sends you an email or text that stirs up difficult, negative feelings in you, wait at least an hour (if possible) before responding. Give yourself a chance to sit with your emotions, and give yourself time to think of a positive response.

Spend Less Time With Negative People

Mindfully choosing to recognize and deal with negativity will make you considerably happier. If you have to work or live with negative people, you have no other choice if you want more peace and less stress in your life.

On the other hand, you might want to think about spending less time with negative people. For example, you can't order your coworkers to leave your company, but you can reduce the amount of time you spend with toxic friends and acquaintances.

Being mindful doesn't mean you have to tolerate bad behavior. If the people in your life drag you down, it might be time to make a few changes. Focus instead on surrounding yourself with people who make you feel peaceful, happy to be alive, and accepted for who you are.

It may come as a shock to realize that those closest to you are draining your energy. Moving toward a more mindful life can be tough because it involves facing unpleasant truths about your relationships, and this can be painful. Just by paying attention to your body and feelings, you'll quickly realize who is worthy of your time, and who treats you like a garbage disposal plant.

Gratitude & Negativity

Negative people focus on what is going wrong in their lives, which creates a sense of dissatisfaction. This is why gratitude practices are useful if you're trying to kick the negativity habit.

This exercise is based on something you do every day, which makes it easy to slot into your regular routine.

Mindfulness Exercise: Grateful "Thank you's"

Over the course of an average day, many of us say "thank you" several times. For example, you probably say "Thanks" when a colleague makes you a coffee or when your partner cleans up after dinner. But do you feel grateful when you say thank you, or has it become somewhat automatic?

The next time you say thank you, pay attention to why you are thanking the other person and take the opportunity to feel gratitude. For example, if your partner does the dishes, take a few seconds to be grateful that they are willing to pitch in with day-to-day chores. If your friend gets you a coffee, take a moment to feel grateful that you get to spend time with a kind, generous person.[27]

If you aren't going to say "thank you" to anyone in the near future, you can try the next practice instead.

Mindfulness Exercise: Take Five

When you next feel frustrated or overwhelmed, grab a piece of paper and write down five things you are grateful for. If you aren't sure where to start, just take a look around. Do you have access to washing facilities? Clean water? Nutritious food? That's three things right there. With a little effort, you'll be able to think of dozens more.

Do you feel reluctant or angry when you try this exercise? That's okay. Maybe you can't help focusing on what's going wrong in your life. Perhaps you think that a gratitude exercise can't possibly make you feel any better, or that everything is too hard and there is nothing to be thankful for.

Do it anyway. It only takes five minutes, and what have you got to lose? Give it a few tries; studies have proven that gratitude practices help most people feel better. Psychologists have found that grateful people are happier and more hopeful, and people who take time to reminisce about fond memories tend to be more content.[28]

MINDFULNESS & EMOTIONAL INTELLIGENCE

Mindfulness enhances your emotional intelligence, or EQ. People with high EQs are skilled in identifying and handling their feelings. They are also adept at picking up on other people's emotions and cheering them up if they're feeling low. By learning how to face and sit with your negative emotions, you'll be able to acknowledge and deal with tough situations and setbacks.

Emotionally intelligent people are more likely to take risks because they know they can handle fear and disappointment. They go beyond their comfort zones and embrace challenge and change. Just think how your career and relationships would change if you no longer felt afraid of fear itself.

Research shows a clear link between mindfulness, EQ, positive mood, and life satisfaction.[29] Psychologists believe that mindful people are more aware of their moods, which helps them choose how best to handle them.

Facing up to your own feelings can also help you channel them in a healthy way. For example, if you are mindful of your own feelings, you might decide that a workout would help you let go of your anger.[30] You'll start making healthier choices, which will have a powerful knock-on effect in every area of your life.

Summary

- Some stress can be a positive force, but too much is a health risk.
- Mindfulness helps you monitor your body and mind for signs of stress, prompting you to face the problem before it gets out of hand.
- Mindfulness can protect you against burnout.
- Sitting with, and accepting your negative emotions can make them seem less overwhelming.

- Mindfulness helps shield you from other people's negativity.
- Cultivating mindfulness will automatically improve your EQ because you will learn how to tune into your feelings.

CHAPTER 5:

MINDFULNESS & ANGER MANAGEMENT

There's nothing wrong with getting angry, or even furious, when the situation warrants it. Anger inspires us to defend ourselves and correct injustice. However, too much anger takes its toll on your mind, body, and relationships.

If you have an anger problem, mindfulness practice will help you learn how to spot the warning signs that your anger is spinning out of control.

ANGER DOESN'T ALWAYS COME FROM THE OUTSIDE

The commonsense view is that anger is triggered by external events. For example, if you think you lost your job for no reason other than your boss dislikes you, you may be angry. If someone cuts you off in traffic, you may feel mad.

However, anger can also stem from a loss of joy. Psychologist Stephen Dansiger, who specializes in anger management, points out that no mood state is permanent. It's unrealistic to expect that we can be happy or relaxed all the time. Unfortunately, some people find this hard to accept, and their disappointment may manifest itself as frustration or anger.[31] Dansiger notes that these individuals feel a sense of loss when feelings of contentment or joy pass, especially if they have a generally unhappy disposition, and this manifests as irritability.

SO, HOW DOES MINDFULNESS HELP?

Mindfulness helps you check in with your body, detect the early signs of anger, and respond to the situation in a way that doesn't harm you or others.

Mindfulness Exercise: How Angry Are You?

If you know or suspect that you have an anger management problem, start by checking in with yourself every two to three hours. All you need to do is set aside a couple of minutes to tune into your mind and body.

Ask yourself the following questions:

1. On a scale of 1-10, with 10 representing an extreme level of anger, how angry am I right now?
2. How does my body feel?
3. What emotions am I feeling right now?
4. What thoughts are going through my head?

This practice helps you detach from your emotions, which makes it easier to remain calm. Remember, anger itself isn't the problem; it's when we start identifying with our anger that we run into trouble.

Mindfulness Exercise: RAIN

This practice, developed by teacher Michele McDonald, can be used to handle any difficult emotion. It is especially useful for taming anger.

RAIN stands for Recognize, Allow, Investigate, and Nurture.

1. **Recognize:** Begin by giving yourself permission to feel your anger. Label it. If you are alone, speak aloud. Tell yourself, "I am angry." Scan your body; do you notice any sensations that signal anger? For example, is your breathing shallow? Have you curled your hands into fists?

2. **Allow:** Hold your anger. Let it just be there. Don't try to reason it away. Whatever your thoughts and feelings, accept them exactly as they are. If you can sit with your anger, you'll learn that it doesn't have to overwhelm you.

3. **Investigate:** Only after you've recognized and felt your anger can you explore what triggered it. Take an attitude of gentle curiosity; there's no need to beat yourself up for being angry. Ask what happened immediately before you feel fury bubble up inside you.

    You don't have to make psychological breakthroughs every time you do the RAIN exercise but, over time, you'll start noticing your personal anger patterns. For example, you might notice that you are quick to get angry when you think someone has failed to respect your authority.

Discovering your triggers gives you an advantage. Depending on the situation, you might be able to avoid triggers, but in most cases, you will need to learn how to work with them. This may mean challenging your assumptions (e.g. "Everyone should respect my authority at all times, and if they don't, it's terrible!") or working on your emotional intelligence (e.g. learning to be more patient towards others.)

4. **Nurture:** Anger is often a sign that your needs are going unmet. For instance, suppose you are angry because your mother doesn't seem interested when you tell her about the problems you are having in your marriage. Your anger may stem from the fact that she isn't offering the kind of nurturing parental love that you want and need.

However angry you may be, you deserve self-compassion, not condemnation. You also need to learn how to nurture yourself when others cannot or will not provide you with love and support. Self-care is an essential part of the RAIN exercise. Have a bath or shower, do some exercise, mindfully eat your favorite food, or do something else that makes you feel good. Congratulate yourself for taking responsibility for your feelings.

Any Progress Is Great!

If you frequently get angry, cut yourself some slack when you do these exercises. Your anger won't disappear immediately. You'll probably still feel frustrated, even when the most intense emotions have passed. That's OK. Getting angry is a learned behavior, and changing an old habit is difficult. You deserve lots of praise for trying a new approach.

GET MINDFUL ABOUT YOUR THOUGHT PATTERNS

Mindfulness gives you the space to play detective, and this can be really useful in understanding your personal anger patterns. The next time you get angry, watch your thoughts. Remember, you don't have to argue with them or wish them away. Reframe them; instead of things that make your life difficult, try to see your thoughts as clues to your anger patterns.[32]

Do you notice any of the following thoughts pop up when you get angry?

Blaming: Do you shift responsibility onto other people? For instance, do you catch yourself saying things like "It's her fault" or "He always makes me mad"?

The truth is that no one can "make" you mad. You have a choice. You can respond to a situation mindfully and handle your anger in a mindful way. You do not have to identify with your anger.

Over-generalizing: Do you use words like "never" or "always"? For example, do you say things like "You never listen to what I have to say" or "You always try to bring me down"?

These statements are rarely true, and they only escalate the tension between you and someone else. Be mindful of the language you use. If you have a problem with someone else's behavior, identify exactly how they are triggering your anger.

Using "should": Do you feel as though people should act fairly towards you at all times? Do you think they have a duty to always act reasonably, to always include you in their activities, and to value your opinion?

Although this would be nice, it just isn't how the world works. "Shoulding" will keep you miserable and trapped by your own unrealistic expectations.

Mind-reading: Do you assume that you "just know" what someone else is thinking? Do you catch yourself thinking things like "I know that he gets angry with me" or "I know that she doesn't think I'm up to the job"?

Unless someone tells us exactly what they're thinking, it's dangerous to assume that we know what's going through their minds. Assumptions can lead to unnecessary argument and misunderstandings.

Don't beat yourself up if you notice yourself blaming, over-generalizing, "shoulding," or mind-reading. Everyone falls into these traps sometimes. The trick is to spot your thinking errors and realize that you don't have to identify with them. Instead, you can choose to use tools like RAIN to respond in a healthier way.

GRUDGES, PAST HURTS, & RELEASING ANGER

So far, we've looked at how you can use mindfulness to deal with angry outbursts and isolated events that make you see red. But what about grudges and long-term grievances? It's worth addressing old hurts because they can cause needless pain for decades if left to fester.

Mindfulness Practice: Using Mindful Visualization To Release Anger

This exercise helps you let go of simmering resentment. You can use it as a tool for forgiveness, or simply as a way of releasing frustration and rage when your anger flares up.

1. Find a quiet place where you will be undisturbed for several minutes.
2. Close your eyes and imagine a peaceful scene, preferably outdoors. You could choose a meadow, a forest, or a beach.
3. When an angry thought pops up, imagine encasing it inside a large pink bubble. Visualize the thought inside the bubble. Feel a sense of relief as you realize that it can't harm you.
4. Picture the bubble floating off into the sky until it is out of sight.

Be Willing To See Change In Other People

Living in the present helps you make a fresh start in your relationships because you can see someone as they are now, not as a shadowy figure who hurt you in the past. People can and do change. You've decided to change by picking up this book and taking steps toward a more mindful life, so you know it's true!

Sometimes, someone will suddenly develop an interest in personal development, often after a major transition like an illness or milestone birthday. Others change gradually over time. They might mellow with age, or slowly shift their priorities and goals.

Either way, try to stay open to the possibility of reconciliation. This doesn't mean you have to forgive and forget. Neither does it mean you should rekindle a relationship with someone who has abused or mistreated you. In some cases, it's best to cut all contact forever. On the other hand, if your grievance is relatively minor and a lot of time has passed, why not try casting your assumptions aside?

When To Seek Help

These exercises can go a long way to resolving pathological anger, but they are no substitute for professional help. If your anger is disrupting your relationships or career, it's best to make an appointment with a doctor or therapist as soon as possible. Most mental health professionals are happy to use mindfulness as part of a treatment plan, so you'll be able to combine these practices with other interventions.

Summary

- Anger is not an intrinsically bad emotion, but too much can harm you and those around you.
- Mindfulness practices can help you identify anger in your body, accept it, and release it.
- Identifying your personal anger patterns can help you overcome thinking errors.
- Staying mindful can help you appreciate positive change in other people.
- You can use mindfulness when working with a mental health professional who specializes in anger management.

CHAPTER 6:

DEPRESSION & MINDFULNESS

Depression is a complex illness. It can be caused by genetics, upbringing, and negative life events, but each case is unique. However, despite their differences, people diagnosed with depression seem to think in similar ways. Their thought patterns are unhelpful and destructive, keeping them locked in a cycle of misery.

According to the National Health Service (NHS), symptoms of depression include:[33]

- Low mood or sadness
- Feeling hopeless and helpless
- Low self-esteem
- Feeling guilt-ridden
- Feeling irritable and intolerant of others
- Having no motivation or interest in things
- Finding it difficult to make decisions

You may also notice physical symptoms, such as aches and pains, and social symptoms, such as a reluctance to spend time with family and friends.

Depression can be classified as "mild," "moderate," or "severe." The more severe your depression, the greater its impact on your daily functioning.

THE LINK BETWEEN THOUGHTS & MOODS

You don't have to believe everything you think. You have the power to start seeing thoughts for what they are – just thoughts – and making healthier choices that help you build a happier life.

Professor Mark Williams, a mindfulness expert and previous director of the Oxford-based Mindfulness Center, puts it this way:

"Gradually, we can train ourselves to notice when our thoughts are taking over and realize that thoughts are simply 'mental events' that do not have to control us."[34]

AARON BECK & COGNITIVE THERAPY

Back in the 1960s, a psychiatrist called Aaron T. Beck was researching depression. He was interested in how his depressed patients thought, not just how they felt. He realized that depressed people tended to:

- Have negative thoughts about themselves
- Have negative thoughts about the world
- Have negative thoughts about the future[35]

His research with depressed people made one thing clear – your thoughts shape your mood. Just like the Buddha, Beck found that when people get caught up in their thoughts and emotional reactions, they are at risk of slipping into an anxious, tense, or otherwise uncomfortable state of mind.

Aaron Beck's Approach To Dealing With Negative Thoughts

Beck believed that depressed people needed to challenge their unhelpful thoughts. His logic went like this: If holding negative thoughts keeps depression going, then replacing them with new, more realistic thoughts should help improve a person's mood.

Beck invented a new form of therapy, Cognitive Therapy (CT), to help his patients fight back against their unhelpful thoughts. He worked with them to uncover their irrational thinking and replace their unhelpful thoughts with more positive statements.

For example, a CT therapist might ask their client to record the thoughts that went through their mind the last time they felt their mood take a dive. The client might record the thought, "Nothing I ever do is good enough." As Aaron Beck would point out, this is an example of a negative thought about the self.

Once the client had identified this thought, the therapist would then work with them to challenge it, using logic and reason. For instance, they might help the client think of times they have succeeded in meeting challenges. The therapist and client might work to come up with a new belief, such as "I am capable of succeeding sometimes, and my work is often good enough."

Critics of CT say that the average person has so many thoughts throughout the day that it's unrealistic to expect them to challenge each and every one. There is no agreement among CT therapists on how many times you need to challenge them before you can expect to see improvement. What's more, if you are depressed, you might not have the mental energy to argue with your thoughts.

The Mindful Alternative

Mindfulness practitioners agree that our thoughts do maintain our emotional states. They also agree that depressed people usually think in particular ways. However, they disagree with Beck on one key point. Instead of just challenging unhelpful thoughts, they believe depressed people also need to learn how to sit with unpleasant feelings.

We're going to look at how mindfulness practices can help alleviate the symptoms of depression. You'll find that other chapters in this book indirectly address symptoms not covered here. For example, irritability is a common sign of depression, so you may find the chapter on anger management useful.

Depression sucks the joy from almost all situations. For instance, you might be spending time with your partner or kids, but feel very little joy. This makes you feel even more depressed. You start thinking, "If I can't even enjoy these special times, what's the point in carrying on?"

Mindfulness exercises can put you back in touch with your own capacity to experience excitement and pleasure.

This starts an upwards spiral; you remember what joy feels like, which inspires you to keep trying to find happiness in everyday situations, which makes you happier, and so on. All the exercises in this book will help you find your way back to the present moment and, as a result, increase your pleasure in living.

Please note: Although mindfulness has been shown to help with symptoms of depression, these practices are not a substitute for personalized medical advice or treatment. If you are depressed or suspect you have depression, work with your regular doctor or therapist to treat your condition.

Depression, Concentration, & Focus

An inability to concentrate is a common symptom of depression. Sufferers find it difficult to read books, follow TV shows, complete tasks at work, or even take part in everyday conversations.

It's not merely a nuisance; it's downright scary when your brain is wrapped in a thick fog. This is why many depressed people retreat from the world. Even when they want to take part in activities, they often feel cut off from everyone, which itself is depressing.

Fortunately, mindfulness has been proven to enhance concentration. For example, research shows that practicing mindfulness regularly for only 7 weeks is likely to improve your attention span, which can make a big difference in your quality of life.[36]

The following practice is a great way to train your attention span. Do it for a few minutes every day, and you should notice improvements quickly.

Mindfulness Exercise: Counting To 10

1. Sit or lie down in a comfortable position.
2. Take a few deep breaths in and out, keeping your attention on your breathing.
3. As you breathe in, count "One."
4. As you exhale, count "Two."
5. Continue until you reach "Ten."
6. If you notice your mind wandering off, bring it back to the present, and start over.

This sounds simple, but it may take a lot of practice before you can count all the way up to ten. Stick with it. Within a few days, it will start to get easier.

Depression, Gratitude, & "Counting Your Blessings"

When you're depressed, the world is a bleak place. You might find that you focus on the suffering you see around you or the upsetting stories you hear on the news. Gratitude practices affirm that there is still hope and kindness, even when everything feels unbearable. They can inspire moments of peace and even joy, however fleeting.

Don't confuse this with the old cliché, "count your blessings." There's a subtle yet important distinction here.

Counting your blessings usually means rattling off a list of things and people in your life, whereas gratitude practice entails slowing down and mindfully appreciating your resources and relationships. People tell you to count your blessings as a means of just brushing off difficulties and struggles. Mindfulness is the opposite; it enables you to accept whatever is going on in your life.

What's more, gratitude practice doesn't involve guilt. You don't need to beat yourself up for being unhappy with your life or wanting to make changes. All you need to do is show up, sit quietly, and acknowledge what you have. Being grateful doesn't mean that you stop noticing your problems, and it definitely isn't a cure for depression. However, it is an effective tool that can help you lead a more mindful life.

Mindfulness Exercise: Gratitude

Start by reflecting on the positive things in your life. Think small. Give thanks for the clean water in your glass, the shoes on your feet, and so on.

Next, reflect on things that are not necessarily good, but may offer you opportunities for growth. For example, you may have been facing problems at work, but your difficulties might encourage you to search for a new, more satisfying position.

Skeptical? When you're depressed, that's understandable. You might be encouraged to know that research shows gratitude exercises can make a big difference. Gratitude reduces feelings of depression, boosts overall wellbeing, and improves sleep quality.[37] You'll feel the benefits within a couple of sessions.

Mindfulness, Acceptance, & Releasing Guilt

If you've ever had depression, you're probably all too familiar with the following phrases:

"What have you got to be depressed about?"

"Count your blessings!"

"There are people out there with real problems. Get over yourself."

This kind of "advice" doesn't help. It actually worsens the situation, because it makes you feel guilty for feeling depressed in the first place. Depression can also make you feel guilty because it encourages you to think about the past. You quickly find yourself getting mad at your past self.

Mindfulness teaches you to accept your depression for what it is. Having depression doesn't make you a bad or ungrateful person. It means you are struggling with a mental health problem that affects millions of people. Through mindfulness, you can gain insight into your thought processes and come to acknowledge that they have no bearing on your worth as a person.

To recover from depression, you need to show yourself some compassion. If you are battling negative thoughts and feel bad about yourself on a daily basis, this is a big challenge! The good news is that it becomes easier with practice.

A Mindfulness Exercise For Self-Compassion

This is a quick, simple practice for those times you are tempted to judge yourself harshly.[38]

1. When you catch yourself thinking self-critical thoughts, make a conscious decision to pause.
2. Decide that you are going to take a few moments to be mindful.
3. Gently place your hand over your heart.
4. Slowly take a few breaths. Watch your breathing. If your mind continues to chatter away, just watch it. Avoid arguing with it.
5. Let yourself feel emotional pain. Acknowledge that you are suffering.

When you are in the depths of depression, trying to do this exercise whenever you judge yourself isn't realistic because depressed people put themselves down with alarming frequency. Just try your best. Aim to do it a few times per day.

Depression & Your Self-Image

Depressed people don't feel good about themselves. If you have a nasty inner critic, it's hard to appreciate yourself. That horrible little voice will highlight all of your supposed flaws and mistakes. A poor self-image and low self-esteem helps keep the cycle of depression going. When you see yourself as a terrible person, you'll conclude that you aren't worthy of time or help.

Depression makes you see the world through a grey filter. You stop appreciating or even noticing the things you do well, and dwell on the bad stuff instead. Over time, you start constructing an image of yourself as inferior and flawed. Mindfulness can help break the cycle by giving you a healthy degree of distance from your emotions.

Practicing the self-compassion exercise above can help because it encourages self-acceptance. The following exercise works in a different way, by capturing your negative self-talk and helping you detach yourself from it.

Mindfulness Exercise: "I'm Having The Thought That…"

The next time you notice a self-deprecating thought, add, "I'm having the thought that…" in front of it.

For instance, if you catch yourself thinking, "I'm so lazy, I'll never get anything done," tell yourself, "I'm having the thought that I'm so lazy and I'll never get anything done." The thought may or may not disappear, but you'll have achieved your objective – it won't feel quite so personal. Remember, don't try to argue with the thought. Your mission is to notice, reframe, and sit with it.

As you continue on with your mindfulness journey, your self-esteem will gradually start to improve. Taking responsibility for yourself is empowering. Knowing that you are taking steps to boost your quality of life will bolster your self-image as someone in control of their destiny.

PREVENTING RELAPSE WITH MINDFULNESS-BASED COGNITIVE THERAPY (MBCT)

Mindfulness-Based Cognitive Therapy (MBCT) is an extension of traditional CT. It helps people recognize unhelpful thinking styles and learn to accept and explore them without judgment. MBCT is particularly useful for people who have had three or more previous episodes of depression.[39]

Zindel Segal, one of the founders of MBCT, points out that depression has a tendency to come back. Whereas CT practitioners focus on helping a client move on from their current period of depression, MBCT has been specially designed to help them stay well.

According to Segal, people who have recovered from depression are easily triggered to relapse when they experience a sad mood or negative thoughts. Depression appears to sensitize the brain to further episodes.

The answer? By staying mindful to shifts in mood and negative thoughts, people can prevent themselves from spiraling into another episode. MBCT techniques aren't designed to stop people from feeling sad, because ups and downs are a normal part of life. Instead, MBCT helps people learn to accept their emotions.[40]

MBCT Exercises

MBCT is usually taught as an eight-week group therapy program. However, you can still enjoy the benefits by practicing MBCT exercises by yourself.

MBCT Exercise #1: The 3-Minute Breathing Space

As the name implies, this exercise takes three minutes. You could set a timer on your phone to chime every sixty seconds. The practice can stand alone, or it makes a good "warm-up" exercise for a longer mindfulness training session.

During the first minute, ask yourself this question: "How am I right now?" Notice any sensations, feelings, and thoughts that arise in your mind and body.

During the second minute, simply follow your breath. Notice the rise and fall of your chest. Notice the temperature of the air.

During the final minute, move your attention from your breath outwards so that you are noticing sensations throughout your body.

MBCT Exercise #2: Mindful Dishwashing

Washing the dishes is an excellent opportunity to use all your senses and ground yourself in the moment. As you wash a plate, notice how the water and soap feel against your skin. Look at how the water and suds slide around the plate, and how the sponge or cloth removes the debris. Hear the sloshing of the water. You may be able to smell or taste the scent or perfume of detergent in the air. With practice, this mundane task can become a rewarding part of your day.

Summary

- If you are suffering from depression, you probably experience a lot of negative thoughts about yourself and the world.
- Some therapists believe that challenging these thoughts is important, but mindfulness practitioners believe that learning to accept them is more effective.
- Mindfulness-Based Cognitive Therapy (MBCT) works by reducing rumination and preventing the kind of downward spiral that can lead to depression.
- Mindfulness can also help people with depression release guilt and shame, grow their self-compassion, improve their self-image, and enjoy brief moments of pleasure.

CHAPTER 7:

MINDFULNESS EXERCISES FOR ANXIETY & PANIC ATTACKS

People who can keep their attention on the present moment rarely experience anxiety. They acknowledge that the future may be unpleasant, but they aren't caught up in the pain of anticipating it. They are free to appreciate the present. Mindfulness training can reduce worry and fear.[41]

In this chapter, you'll learn how mindfulness can help you cope with the symptoms of anxiety. Note that mindfulness in general is good for anyone suffering from anxiety disorders. However, the techniques in this chapter are especially effective for people who feel too anxious to even attempt mindfulness exercises. We'll also look at how mindfulness can help you deal with panic attacks.

What Is Anxiety?

Anxiety is a feeling of fear, worry, or general unease. Some anxiety is normal and healthy. If we didn't get anxious about potentially dangerous situations or serious problems, we might not prepare for them properly. For example, feeling anxious before an important test can give you an edge and help you get a better grade.

On the other hand, chronic or severe anxiety wreaks havoc on your body and mind. If your anxiety starts affecting your life – for example, if you are so worried or nervous that you can't get your work done – you may have an anxiety disorder.

Psychological symptoms of excessive anxiety include being irritable, feeling uneasy most of the time, difficulty sleeping, feeling as though you could cry at any moment, and seeking more reassurance than usual from other people. You may also experience physical symptoms, such as feeling faint, a loss of appetite, an upset stomach, headaches, and palpitations.

CAN YOU BE TOO ANXIOUS TO PRACTICE MINDFULNESS?

If you are very anxious, mindfulness might feel completely impossible. For example, you may try to sit down and observe your breathing for a few moments, but feel your anxiety rising until it feels unbearable. Self-critical thoughts, such as "I can't do this right" and "This is just making me too worried" start creeping in.

Fortunately, you can ease yourself into mindfulness by working on self-compassion. Psychologist Mitch Ablett suggests that people with high anxiety can use the following practice as a bridge to meditation and other mindfulness exercises.[42]

Mindfulness Exercise: Self-Compassion Mindfulness For Anxiety

1. Sit upright in a comfortable chair. It doesn't matter whether you keep your eyes closed or open.
2. Acknowledge that you are suffering from anxiety. Tell yourself out loud, "I'm acknowledging that I'm in a lot of emotional pain. My suffering is real."
3. Take a single deep breath. Notice how it feels to inhale then exhale.
4. Affirm your pain again. This time, say "I'm caring for myself."
5. Repeat step #3, but this time focus on two breathing cycles.
6. Tell yourself, "This is hard for me. I accept that."
7. Try to observe three breathing cycles.
8. Again, acknowledge that the practice is challenging. Tell yourself that your pain is real and that your practice is a form of self-care.

Repeat this practice as many times as you like. At first, completing it once will be tough, and that's okay. A few minutes is all you need. After a few sessions, you'll begin to notice the difference.

Showing self-compassion is a great first step when you have anxiety. The next practice uses drawing as a grounding exercise. If you struggle to remain still during your mindfulness sessions, it's a great alternative to conventional seated practices.

Mindfulness Exercise: Drawing Mandalas

You've probably seen mandala coloring books for adults, or even tried one yourself. Their creators claim that coloring the patterns is relaxing and can relieve stress and anxiety. Buddhists would agree; the ancient practice of drawing and coloring mandalas has long been used as a form of meditation.[43]

Mandalas are abstract designs, usually circular, made up of geometric forms, organic shapes, or both. They can be left plain or colored. A mandala has an identifiable central point. Their shapes and forms radiate outward. In Sanskrit, the word "mandala" means "circle."

Follow these steps to draw your own mandalas:

1. Find a square piece of paper. It can be whatever size you like.
2. Draw a small dot in the center of the paper. You can use a ruler to check the positioning.
3. Draw three or four concentric circles. Every circle should have the dot at its center.
4. Let your intuition guide you when drawing your mandala. The only rule is that it should be symmetrical. Mandalas are repetitive, which is one reason they are psychologically soothing. Keep the colors symmetrical too.
5. You can add color as you go, or wait until you have completed your design before adding it.
6. As you draw, notice the sensation of the pencil or pen in your hand. Notice how lines and color appear on the page. What does it feel like to make contact with the paper?

If you make a mistake, don't beat yourself up. You don't need to produce a perfect work of art; the aim is to focus your attention on the act of drawing. When you are engrossed in creating a mandala, your mind is less likely to stray to thoughts that make you anxious.

You may even experience a flow state whilst drawing and coloring. During a flow state, you become completely engrossed in whatever you are doing. You forget where you are, and time seems to fly by. You never have to watch the clock, and your mind effortlessly focuses on the task in front of you.

By definition, you can't force yourself into a flow state. See it as a nice side-effect rather than a goal, and simply appreciate it.

Mindfulness For Panic Attacks

Panic attacks are overwhelming with sudden feelings of anxiety combined with physical symptoms. During an attack, your body releases stress hormones, including cortisol and adrenaline. These cause symptoms like nausea, irregular breathing, palpitations, sweating, and lightheadedness. Panic attacks last up to half an hour, but most peak within ten minutes. They sometimes have a clear trigger, but they can also happen for no obvious reason.

The good news is that panic attacks aren't harmful. Unfortunately, if you don't learn how to handle them, they can start to take over your life. For example, if you experience a panic attack, you might start to worry about suffering further attacks in the future. Ironically, this can make them more likely to happen, and the cycle continues.

Mindful approaches to panic attacks are becoming more popular among mental health professionals. Instead of distracting yourself from an attack, try sitting with – or even embracing – the sensations.

Mindfulness Exercise: Sitting With A Panic Attack

1. The next time you detect the beginnings of a panic attack, pause and take a deep breath. Tell yourself, "Ah, here we go. This is a panic attack."
2. Remind yourself that your symptoms always pass.
3. Adopt an attitude of curiosity rather than resistance. Notice your physical symptoms. Label them. For example, "sweaty palms," "chest tightness," and so on.
4. Watch your symptoms reach their peak. Usually, this will be at the ten-minute mark.

This exercise will help you accept what is happening in your body. When you decide to experience a panic attack instead of reacting with more panic, it might even pass more quickly than usual.

Mindfulness Exercise: Say "STOP!"

Here's an exercise you can do whenever you start feeling overwhelmed by worry. With practice, you can use it to delay panic attacks or prevent them entirely.

STOP stands for Slow down, Take a breath, Observe, and Proceed.[44]

1. Stop. Whatever you are doing, pause. Move away from your desk, put your phone down, or find someplace to sit.
2. Take a breath. If you are experiencing racing thoughts, say "In" with each inhalation, and "Out" every time you exhale.
3. Observe. Consider how your body feels. Label your emotions. Step back and notice the thoughts racing through your head. Remember that your thoughts and feelings don't always represent reality.
4. Proceed. Pick an activity that will give you a psychological boost. For example, you could call a friend for support or make yourself a hot drink.

BEFRIENDING ANXIETY

Harvard psychology professor Ron Siegel recommends that people with anxiety go one step further. He says that not only should you learn how to "ride out" waves of anxiety, but actually induce it. By deliberately triggering anxious feelings, you can practice letting them pass through you. This exercise is powerful because it teaches you that all anxiety passes eventually.

Mindfulness Exercise: Inducing Anxiety[45]

1. Sit quietly and scan your body for signs of tension or anxiety.

2. If you can locate any feelings of anxiety, such as a knot in your stomach, allow yourself to notice it.
3. If not, intentionally bring to mind a situation or person who makes you afraid or worried. Choose something that makes you apprehensive rather than terrified.
4. Breathe deeply and acknowledge your fear.
5. It won't be long before your mind wanders off. When this happens, return to the anxious feeling. You'll soon notice that maintaining a state of anxiety is actually quite difficult. Even when you want it to stick around, it fades within a few minutes.

Working With Your Doctor

Mindfulness definitely works well for lots of people who have to deal with anxiety. On the other hand, it's not a cure-all. You'll need to make lifestyle changes and possibly work with a doctor or therapist to make a full recovery. Eating a good diet, getting plenty of exercise, and working on your relationships usually make up the other pieces of the puzzle.

If your symptoms are having a major impact on your life, or self-help measures don't appear to be working, it's time to consult a mental health professional. Your regular physician will be able to point you in the right direction. Doctors and therapists are starting to appreciate the power of mindfulness, so they will probably be happy to help you incorporate it as part of a treatment plan.

Summary

- Mindfulness grounds you in the present, so it is useful for anyone who worries and ruminates.
- Mindful drawing is a longstanding tradition that can alleviate anxiety and stress.
- Mindfulness can help you cope with a panic attack because it has a grounding effect.
- Mindfully inducing anxiety teaches you that anxiety doesn't last forever. This is an empowering concept.
- If you are too anxious to try mindfulness practices, acknowledging this anxiety can be a great help.
- If anxiety is interfering with your life and self-help isn't working, consult a doctor.

CHAPTER 8:

BUILDING BETTER HABITS WITH MINDFULNESS

Never underestimate the power of habit. Much of our day-to-day lives, including the thoughts we have about ourselves and others, are shaped by repetition. The more you repeat a habit, the harder it is to shake.

In this chapter, we'll look at how you can conquer undesirable habits using mindfulness. We'll also talk about ways you can use mindfulness to build new, healthy habits that will help you meet your life goals.

Not all habits are harmful. Brushing your teeth in the morning is a habit, as is washing your hands after you use the bathroom. Good habits keep you aligned with your higher goals and objectives. In this case, tooth brushing and handwashing steer you on the right path to your goal of leading a healthy life. It's only when our habits prevent us from fulfilling our potential that they become a problem.

OVERCOMING "BAD" HABITS

We all know what we mean when we talk about "bad habits." Smoking, drinking too much, watching too much TV, and interrupting others are common examples. The problem with this phrase is that it invites judgment. By labeling a behavior as "bad," we're affirming to ourselves that our behavior is fundamentally wrong. This isn't a helpful way to talk to ourselves, because it triggers self-criticism. And, as we know, criticizing ourselves isn't constructive.[46]

Instead, refer to habits that disrupt your life or stop you achieving your goals as "unhelpful" or "unhealthy." It may seem like a subtle difference, but changing your vocabulary encourages a more compassionate attitude, which can help you choose healthier habits. Unhealthy habits don't make you a bad person. We all have them!

Mindfulness Exercise: Identifying Unhealthy Habits

The first step to conquering unhealthy habits is to identify them. Over the next few days, make a note whenever you catch yourself engaging in habit-driven behavior that doesn't align with your values. For instance, if you value efficiency and achievement, compulsively checking your email every ten minutes is an unhelpful habit that doesn't serve you.

Ask yourself how you feel when you engage in this habit. Do you feel physical discomfort, emotional discomfort, or both? Pretend you are a scientist or anthropologist. Act as a neutral witness rather than a critic. How does this habit prevent you from leading the kind of life you want to live?

Some habits, such as smoking, are always harmful. However, other habits don't fall into the same category. For example, consider excessive internet use and overeating. Unlike smoking, using the internet and eating are not intrinsically unhealthy behaviors. It's only when you start to abuse them that the trouble starts. You can't stop eating, and it's unrealistic to cut the internet out of your life, but you can learn to take a mindful approach and moderate your behavior.

Why Habits Are So Hard To Break

So, you've identified your unhelpful habits and decided to make changes. Unfortunately, as you probably know, it isn't that easy to adopt new behaviors overnight.

To help understand why habits stick like glue, let's look at two complementary theories.

The Dual Operating Systems Theory

Economist Daniel Kahneman has proposed that human beings have two "operating systems" when it comes to making decisions: System 1 and System 2. System 1 is driven by instinct and emotion. It urges us to take immediate action to solve a problem or relieve discomfort. For instance, if you are very thirsty, you will feel an overwhelming compulsion to drink a glass of water if it's placed in front of you.

By contrast, System 2 is based on rational thought. When System 2 takes over, we can think about the long-term effects of our actions.[47]

To put it simply, System 1 creates the urge to engage in unhealthy habits. When you try to suppress a habit, such as biting your nails or reaching for a piece of candy even though you aren't hungry, you are forced to battle against a powerful force that's hard to subdue with willpower.

Sure, you might be able to grit your teeth and fight the urge occasionally, but merely urging yourself to act differently isn't the best solution. As your habit becomes more and more entrenched, your intentions become even less effective.

System 2 relies on the prefrontal cortex, which is the part of the brain responsible for long-term planning. It's the part of your brain that recognizes the cost of indulging in an unhealthy habit or craving. However, you can't depend on your prefrontal cortex to always steer you in the right direction. When you are under stress, it shuts down. The cruel irony is that stress often makes cravings worse, so when you really need your prefrontal cortex, it's not much help.

If you think about it, this shouldn't come as a surprise. For example, perhaps you have experienced "brain freeze" during an exam or said something regrettable during a heated argument with a friend.

While the prefrontal cortex goes quiet under stress, the older parts of the human brain take over. The prefrontal cortex is a relatively recent development in human history. Before it arrives on the scene, our behaviors are controlled by parts of the brain that cause us to act on impulse. The result? When we feel threatened, whether by external or internal events, it's all too easy to give in to our urges. It's only later, when our prefrontal cortex comes back online, that we can reflect on the damage we've done.

THE REWARD CIRCUIT – TRIGGER, BEHAVIOR, REWARD

Psychologist Judson Brewer, a researcher with a special interest in addiction, points out that our brains have evolved to form habits. They operate on the principles of positive and negative reinforcement. If something feels good, you'll want to do it again. If something feels bad, your brain will try to avoid it.[48]

Let's take a simple example. One day, you see a delicious-looking piece of cake – a trigger. Your brain automatically urges you to eat it – a behavior – because it suspects that the cake will taste great. You eat the cake and it does indeed taste fantastic. These sensations are your reward for eating the cake.

Once this process is complete, your brain lays down what psychologists call a context-dependent memory. Your brain creates a new pathway that lets you remember what you just ate – cake – and where you found it. From a survival perspective, this is a wonderful mechanism because it will save you time in the future. You won't have to wonder whether cake tastes good; you'll be drawn to it straight away. This makes the cake harder to resist.

Your brain may then decide that cake may be the answer when you next feel sad, lonely, or otherwise uncomfortable. When you respond to an internal trigger – an uncomfortable feeling – and eat cake, you'll find that you do feel better, just as your brain predicted. Every time you respond to your triggers, you further cement this new habit. Over time, it starts to feel more natural and becomes harder to shift.

So, How Can We Change?

The picture might seem a bit bleak right now, but you can change! You just need to adopt a new, more mindful approach. With regular training, you can change your routine to help you make better choices, you can explore your cravings mindfully, and you can train your prefrontal cortex to help you out during stressful moments.

In brief, you need to:

1. Take a proactive approach to blocking your behaviors.
2. Take an attitude of curiosity, rather than condemnation, when you act on your impulses or cravings.

Notice Your Triggers & Put Up Some Roadblocks

Having investigated your personal triggers, you can make adjustments to your environment or routine that make it easier to practice healthier habits without having to rely on willpower alone.

Some examples:

- If you have a habit of buying candy whenever you visit the grocery store, plan a new route around the store that doesn't take you through the candy aisle.

- If you check your email and social media as soon as you wake up in the morning, start leaving your phone in the kitchen when you go to bed. Get an old-fashioned alarm clock for your bedside table so that you don't need to rely on your phone to wake you up.
- If you automatically switch on the TV as soon as you come home from work, move the TV to another room or store the remote somewhere you can't easily access it.

Persistence is key. Psychologists believe that it takes approximately 66 days to build a new habit.[49] Making big changes requires a lot of effort. Make things easier on yourself by focusing on one or two changes at a time. Don't try to reinvent yourself or your life overnight; you'll become overwhelmed and may give up completely. Remember to congratulate yourself along the way.

A feeling or thought can drive us towards an unhealthy coping mechanism, but we don't have to go along with it. You are not at the mercy of your brain.

Embrace Your Cravings

In Chapter Seven, you learned that leaning into a panic attack instead of resisting it will help your symptoms pass quicker and that deliberately triggering anxiety proves to yourself that you can handle it.

This exercise is based on the same principle.

Mindfulness Exercise: Urge Surfing[50]

1. As soon as you notice a craving or urge, stop what you are doing.

2. Sit or stand still, and get as comfortable as possible.

3. Tune into your body. Where can you feel the craving? Is your body tense? Are you sweating? Describe it in non-judgmental language. For instance, you might say to yourself, "I notice that my mouth is dry, and I am craving a beer."

    If you can't locate the urge in your body, think back to another time you experienced the craving. Close your eyes and bring the memory to life in as much detail as possible. If you are worried that recalling this memory will prompt you to give in to a craving, recall a time you felt the urge but didn't act on it.

4. Having identified the part of your body most strongly associated with your craving, pay close attention to how it feels. Do the sensations change or move around? Could you draw an outline on your body, showing where you feel this sensation?

    Notice any thoughts that pop into your head. For instance, are you trying to argue or bargain with yourself? Watch out for thoughts like "Just don't do it" or "This is terrible! I can't bear this feeling!" Sit with them.

5. Breathe as normal for 1-2 minutes.

6. Return your attention to the part of your body where you are experiencing the craving. Imagine that you are directing your breath towards it. Do the sensations change?

7. Urges tend to come and go in waves. Think of your breath as a surfboard. When a wave hits you, take a big breath in. As it passes, exhale. Tell yourself that you are an expert surfer and that riding the wave is no big deal for you.

8. Within 20-30 minutes, you'll notice that your urge has started to soften.

    Believe it or not, confronting urges can become fun! Judson Brewer points out that curiosity is, in itself, rewarding. You'll start to get a kick out of sitting with your cravings, which is much more constructive than mindlessly giving into your urges or trying to white-knuckle your way through a craving.

Understanding how habits work can also help us be more compassionate and understanding of others. Now that you know how easy it is to form a habit, you might find yourself making (reasonable) allowances for their behavior. You'll be able to relate to them on a deeper level, seeing them as fallible human beings just like you.

When You Slip Up, Show Yourself Some Compassion

You're human, and you will fall back into your old habits at some point. For example, you may have had a particularly stressful day at work, and the idea of surfing an urge for 20 minutes might seem ridiculous when you could grab a chocolate bar or smoke a cigarette instead.

It's okay to be an imperfect person. Reaffirm your commitment to making changes and aim to be mindful next time around. Mindfulness will become a healthy habit and get easier the more you practice.

Summary

- Our habits dictate our behaviors and can shape our lives in profound ways.
- Our brains are hardwired to form habits, and they tend to become irrational when under stress.
- Through mindfulness and observation, we can learn to surf cravings and make simple changes to our routines that prevent them from arising in the first place.
- Try to take an attitude of curiosity rather than judgment when working with habits.
- Paying attention to your habits may not come naturally at first, but observing them will eventually become second nature.
- Show yourself compassion when you slip back into unhealthy habits.

CHAPTER 9:

BEATING PROCRASTINATION & BOOSTING PRODUCTIVITY WITH MINDFULNESS

Procrastination isn't merely an annoyance; it can do serious damage to your career, personal life, and self-esteem. In this chapter, we'll look at what procrastination is, why we do it, and how mindfulness can help us get back on track.

What Exactly Does It Mean To Procrastinate?

When we procrastinate, we delay a task. Most people associate procrastination with school and work. None of us are surprised when a student admits that they have been procrastinating instead of studying for a test or writing an essay. At work, we might procrastinate on menial or challenging tasks, such as writing a presentation or drawing up a complex spreadsheet.

However, we also procrastinate in our personal lives. For example, some people vow to lose weight or give up smoking but never seem to get around to it. We can even procrastinate when it comes to relationships. Perhaps you've decided that you want to look for a partner and start dating, for example, but never seem to find the time to join new groups or put up a profile on a dating website.

What Are The Dangers Of Procrastination?

Procrastination also carries health risks. For example, research shows that procrastinators are more likely to get sick. They also suffer higher levels of stress.[51]

Procrastination can also damage your relationships. If you delay making important decisions, such as when to buy a house or start a family, your partner's patience may run out. Procrastinate too much, and your loved one will eventually start questioning whether you really care about the relationship at all.

Why Do We Delay Tasks?

We procrastinate because it offers some kind of pay-off. At first, this seems like a strange idea. Putting off important tasks leads to stress in the end, so why would anyone choose to delay them?

Put simply, procrastination makes you feel better in the short term. Suppose you have to write a long, complicated report at work. It's going to take several days, and the topic is boring. It doesn't sound very appealing, does it? If you tell yourself that you'll do it later, you immediately lower your stress levels. This sends a signal to your brain: "If we delay a task, the tension and stress goes away."

This is why procrastination is best thought of as an unhealthy habit. We get into the habit of responding to a trigger (e.g. a project or essay) with a behavior (delaying the task) that rewards us in some way (a drop in stress levels).

Psychologists have found that low levels of mindfulness are linked to procrastination.[52] People who procrastinate struggle to regulate their behaviors and emotions. This means they find it hard to force themselves to start tasks that are boring or unpleasant. By contrast, mindful individuals are better-equipped to recognize and accept their emotions, even the unpleasant ones, and continue to engage with tasks anyway.

What does this mean for you? If you start using the techniques in this book in your everyday life, you'll be less likely to procrastinate. You'll be able to tolerate discomfort and negative emotions. Tough tasks will still stress you out, but you won't feel the need to delay them so often.

Procrastination & Negative Self-Talk

Sometimes, we procrastinate not just because we don't want to do the task, but because we don't want to endure negative self-talk or self-criticism. If you are in the habit of putting yourself down, you probably speak unkindly to yourself whenever you're facing a challenging task. Therefore, it makes sense that you'd want to avoid doing something that will trigger your inner critic.

For example, let's say you need to paint your living room. Painting a room, particularly if it's large, takes time and effort. But let's also suppose that you have low self-confidence and an active inner critic and you believe that all your DIY projects will end in failure. Painting a large room whilst having to listen to a voice telling you that your efforts are all in vain won't be an enticing prospect under those circumstances.

If you are a chronic procrastinator, you need to figure out whether your self-talk is holding you back. By noticing the way you talk to yourself, you can learn to stop identifying with your critic's harsh words.

Mindfulness Exercise: Noticing Your Inner Critic

1. The next time you find yourself feeling discouraged in the face of a big task or project, take a moment to slow down and check in with yourself.
2. Notice the thoughts racing through your head. Are they negative, positive, or neutral?
3. If you notice a critical voice, what is it like? Is it quiet or loud, male or female, snide or outright aggressive?
4. Every time a new critical thought pops up, label it. Say, "Oh, a critical thought" or "There's a critical voice."
5. Notice that each thought passes. Even if another comes along to take its place, no thought stays around forever.
6. Acknowledge your critic, and then start the task anyway. Take it slow; how could you make some progress in the next five or ten minutes?

There's no need to fight back against the unkind voice in your head. The difference between people who get things done and those who are held back by their insecurities is that the former have learned to acknowledge and accept it.

FINDING PURPOSE AT WORK

Do you ever arrive at work, look at your to-do list, and start asking, "What's the point?" When you're caught up in the daily grind, it's easy to lose your sense of purpose. Over time, you might become demotivated, disengaged, and depressed. You may start to procrastinate. After all, why bother putting in the work if you don't believe in it?

Mindfulness Exercise: Why Are You At Work?

Asking yourself a few questions each morning reminds you why your job is important, renews your sense of purpose, and keeps you focused.

At the start of every working day, ask yourself the following:

"What is my role here?"

"How can I better serve others?"

"What do I need to do today?"

"What must I do first?"

You can adapt these questions to your circumstances if you are a stay at home parent, student, or retiree.

Even if your work is dull and seems unimportant, you can still find some meaning if you look hard enough.

For example, suppose you have a boring entry-level administrative job at a small office. You may not find it easy to see the broader purpose of your role, but look closer.

You may be able to gain some satisfaction from cheering up other workers in your office or reminding yourself that, without your efforts, the business would quickly descend into chaos because no one would be keeping up with the mail. See your efforts as part of a greater whole.

Why You Need To Stop Multitasking

We all like to think that we've mastered the art of doing several tasks at once. For instance, lots of us check our email while eating lunch, carrying on a conversation with a co-worker, and planning what to have for dinner. During the working day, our attention flits back and forth between various projects, phone calls, and so on.

Perhaps you are reading this book while watching a TV show or catching up on your emails. If so, switching off your devices and giving the book your complete attention is a small act of mindfulness in itself. As you continue reading, put the book down if you need to take a moment to think about an idea or exercise. As you read, think about how you could apply these principles in your everyday life.

Multitasking can make you feel productive. Unfortunately, this is just an illusion. Research shows that multitasking lowers your productivity.[53] Contrary to popular opinion, women aren't better at juggling tasks than men; both sexes are much worse off when they try to split their attention in several directions. It's not just a matter of practice, either. People who multitask often are actually worse at it![54]

If you get into the habit of multitasking, you lose your ability to focus long enough to assimilate new information. In other words, multitasking slowly undermines your ability to learn. For example, you can't pick up new information if your attention is split between your phone, your email, and an online article.[55]

Mindfulness & Monotasking

When you make a commitment to complete tasks mindfully, you are forced to slow down and put them in order. Then, you work your way through them, one at a time.

If you find the idea of focusing on a single task at a time uncomfortable, notice your thoughts and feelings. Does monotasking make you feel lazy? Do you feel as though you aren't productive unless you are juggling (or trying to juggle) multiple tasks? Does your body feel tense? Tune in and see what's going on inside.

Still skeptical? Stop multitasking for a week, and see what impact it has on both your professional and personal life.

Tech, Productivity, & Procrastination

Like it or not, technology has become an inescapable part of our lives. Most people assume that it's normal and harmless to spend hours every day glued to a screen, but have you ever stopped to consider the real cost of your tech habits, especially when it comes to your productivity?

It takes only a few moments to get sucked into a rabbit hole. We click an interesting looking link, which takes us to another website, which encourages us to share content on social media, and so on. It never ends!

Even if you only spend a few minutes browsing a website, your brain will be overwhelmed by information. We haven't evolved to cope with the sheer quantity of data that gets pumped into our heads every day, and it's almost impossible to perform well at work if we are distracted by our phones and the internet.

Fear Of Missing Out (FOMO), Envy, & Insecurity

Do you have the feeling that other people are having a much better time than you? Does it seem like everyone else has an easier, more glamorous, and exciting life? You may be experiencing FOMO, a modern condition usually triggered by technology.

Before the rise of the internet, we didn't really have the chance to see what anyone outside our immediate social circle was doing. Now, it's all too easy to keep tabs on them and make comparisons.

If you have FOMO, you probably feel inferior to people on social media. You might feel envious of their jobs, relationships, or possessions. Poring over everyone's posts and photos won't make you feel great about yourself, and it can become a habit.

At worst, FOMO can be lethal. Some people are so worried that they'll miss some key update or post on their social media feed that they can't put their phones down when driving. Others waste so much time comparing themselves to everyone else that they become clinically depressed or anxious.

If you suffer from FOMO, you aren't living in the present. Your real problem isn't that you don't have someone else's "perfect" life. The real problem is that you are missing out on your own.

How To Use Tech Mindfully

So, is technology evil? Not at all! It's great for helping us keep in touch with people who matter to us, and it makes work a lot easier. Even if you wanted to, it would be almost impossible to escape it. We just have to figure out how to use technology in a mindful way.

Follow these tips for a healthier relationship with your devices:

Turn off all unnecessary notifications: Notifications interrupt your workflow, so turn them off. If you are worried about missing an interesting notification, acknowledge what's going on in your body and mind. Maybe your muscles feel tense, or perhaps you are experiencing a vague, low-level panic. Notice how it feels to go several hours without using your phone.

Use a tracker to monitor your use: We usually know when we're spending too much time online, but seeing raw data takes your awareness to a new level. There are lots of apps designed to help you lead a more mindful life. You may be in for a shock when you see the numbers!

Be mindful before reacting to people online: What do you do when you see or read something that makes you mad? Next time you start typing a response, pause for a moment and reflect on what you are trying to achieve. Be honest with yourself; what are your true motives?

Be aware that people seldom change their minds online and that fighting with someone usually ends in drama. Can you afford to let yourself be derailed by someone's Facebook or Twitter post?

The next time you are tempted to write an angry comment, notice what that urge feels like. See if you can surf it or wait it out instead of reacting. You'll feel calmer, you'll get more work done – and you won't get into so many pointless arguments.

Use mindfulness to overcome FOMO: Quitting social media is an effective cure for FOMO, but it isn't realistic for most people. If you have family and friends across the globe, there's no sense in cutting all virtual ties just because you've fallen into the habit of over-analyzing everyone else's lives.

So, what's the answer? Fortunately, research shows that being mindful reduces FOMO.[56] Staying aware of your emotions makes you less vulnerable to destructive envy. The next time you feel jealous, insecure, or sad when browsing social media, put your phone down for a moment and feel the emotion in your body. Feel it rise and fall. Breathe deeply. You'll notice that the emotion peaks within a few minutes.

Remind yourself that you have a choice. You are free to keep on browsing social media for hours at a time, but what's really going on? Are you simply addicted to making harmful comparisons, using the internet, or both?

Don't feed someone else's FOMO: When a social media post triggers your FOMO, maybe your first instinct is to post something that impresses your followers.

But take a moment to think about this a little more mindfully. When you participate in internet one-upmanship, be mindful of how your actions affect others. If you want to share photos and stories, do it with a sense of appreciation, gratitude, and joy.

Summary

- Mindful people tend to procrastinate less often.
- We procrastinate when we feel overwhelmed by negative emotions or want to escape our inner critic.
- Mindfully accepting these thoughts and feelings makes tasks more tolerable, thus reducing procrastination.
- Mindful questions can help you locate a sense of purpose.
- Technology is an inescapable part of our lives, and we need to learn to use it mindfully.

CHAPTER 10:

BEATING "WHEN... THEN" SYNDROME WITH MINDFULNESS

So far, you've experimented with lots of mindfulness practices for specific problems like stress and depression. In this chapter, we're going to take a step back and look at the bigger picture. Mindfulness isn't just a useful approach for handling emotions on a day-to-day basis; it is a way of living.

ARE YOU LIVING FOR THE PRESENT OR THE FUTURE?

Do you tell yourself any of the following?

"When I land that new job, then I'll be happy."

"When I finally buy a new home, then I'll be happy."

"When I earn that promotion, then I can relax."

"When I find a partner, then I'll feel better about myself."

"When I lose 30lbs, then I'll feel better about my body."

These are examples of "When...Then" Syndrome in action. The main symptom is an obsession with making as much progress as you can, in the shortest possible amount of time, whilst ignoring what's going on around you.

If you're suffering from this affliction, you'll never be able to accept your life in the present moment. Instead, you'll pour all efforts into chasing whatever you think will make you happy. This is a tragedy because you will deprive yourself of the joys that come with living in the here and now.

Lots of people live like this. In fact, it's normal. If you were to ask your family and friends whether they are happy with their lives, they would probably tell you that they will be a lot happier when they finally manage to make some kind of major change.

Why We Need To Enjoy The Journey

Lots of us assume that we need to wait until we "arrive" at our destination before we feel happy. This perspective leads to nothing but pain. Why?

First, when you pin all your hopes for happiness on a single event or possession, you are vulnerable to disappointment. Few things live up to our expectations. That's just how life works. It's impossible to foresee every eventuality.

To make matters worse, human beings have a special ability to assume, often on an unconscious level, that success in one aspect of their lives will somehow change everything for the better. For example, you might trick yourself into thinking that a new relationship will somehow make you happy and that you will suddenly be able to launch yourself into a new career or finally commit to a diet.

Imagine that you drop dead tomorrow having never achieved your goals. It's a grim thought, isn't it? However, wouldn't it be even worse to die having never experienced life in the present because you were too busy striving towards a distant goal? The brutal truth is that you don't know whether the future will ever arrive. Doesn't it make more sense to focus on learning to live in the here and now?

Finally, by fixating on what you want, you are devaluing what you already have. For example, let's say you are working to get a promotion so that you can buy a bigger house. If you aren't careful, you'll start to slip into a dissatisfied state of mind. You may start feeling resentful that your boss doesn't pay you enough money, or that your current house isn't big enough. These thoughts keep you from slowing down and enjoying your life as it is right now. Given that it's the only life you have, you might as well savor it!

Mindfulness Exercise: How Much Time Do You Spend In The Future?

Today, keep a piece of paper and a pen or pencil on hand. Every time you drift off into a daydream about the future, place a mark on the sheet of paper. At the end of the day, count them up. Are you surprised by how much time you spend time traveling?

Cravings Never End

There is always something new to desire. We set a goal, work towards it, feel happy for a brief time when we meet it – then we start hankering after something new.

Until you realize that material possessions and status will never bring you true contentment, you are trapped in an uncomfortable cycle of striving, achieving, disappointment, more striving, etc. The only way to break free is to learn to live in the present.

Consider this: All your life, you have assumed that a particular person, possession, or title will make you happy. You already know that life doesn't work like that, or you wouldn't still be searching for contentment. Based on your experience so far, why would you think that your next achievement will be the one that really does make you happy?

When you accept that you will always want the next big thing, you are free to choose goals that are actually meaningful to you, and then to pursue them with an attitude of joy and curiosity rather than grim determination.

This isn't easy. We live in a materialistic world dominated by marketing campaigns that tell us the only true path to happiness is achievement and consumption. It takes courage to re-examine your values and go against the grain.

The Hedonic Treadmill

If you are hoping that the "right" car, house, or widescreen TV will finally bring you contentment, you are headed for disappointment. Research has shown that accumulating memories, not material possessions, makes us happier.[57]

There's no doubt that buying gadgets or a new house can make you happy for a while, but we soon become desensitized to new luxuries. The elation wears off, and we start to look ahead to the next thing. This is known as hedonic adaptation, or the hedonic treadmill.

On the other hand, memories last forever, as do the feelings associated with them. If you mindfully enjoy the good times, you can conjure up these memories later and savor them all over again. Sharing experiences with others also strengthens your relationships, which in turn boosts your overall wellbeing and quality of life.

Think twice before investing in a fancy gadget you don't need. If you have some spare cash, why not put it towards an experience or adventure instead, preferably with people you love?

Keep Your Mind & Heart Open

Life isn't predictable. The best-laid plans go awry. The good news is that you have a choice. You can try to keep up the illusion of control, or you can remain open to the idea of multiple possibilities. Think back over your life so far. Have there been times where everything went wrong, yet it worked out well in the end?

For example, you might have been fired from your job, but then found a much better position elsewhere. Or maybe the person you hoped to marry didn't feel the same way, but you later met someone who proved a more suitable match?

Maybe things won't work out as you'd like, but that doesn't mean you can't turn the situation to your advantage. At the very least, you can use disasters and setbacks as your teachers. Tough times are the perfect opportunity to practice your mindfulness skills.

You can feel happy anytime, anywhere, if you fully accept the present moment and engage in the dance of life.

Summary

- Fixating on a future that may or may not arrive means you can't enjoy the present moment.
- Falling short of your goals isn't the worst thing that could happen to you; missing out on your life as it is right now is a greater tragedy.
- Don't make the mistake of assuming that an achievement in one area of your life will magically fix everything else.
- Material possessions make us happy but hedonic adaptation means that these pleasures don't last.
- Be open to what the future may bring, and don't hold too tightly to your expectations.

CHAPTER 11:

STAYING PRESENT WHILE PLANNING THE FUTURE

At this point, you might be thinking along these lines: "Sure, staying in the present helps me live a more joyful life. But I can't stay in the present moment all the time! I've got to think about my future. I've got to make some plans!"

In this chapter, we'll look at how you can strike this delicate balance. You'll learn how to set mindful goals and make positive decisions.

MEDITATION & MINDFULNESS IN THE REAL WORLD

Most of us don't want to sell our houses, give away all our possessions, and move to a remote cave or monastery. We need mindfulness practices that work for ordinary people who lead ordinary lives.

Coach Brad Waters addresses this issue head-on in an article published in *Psychology Today*.[58] He notes that being mindful doesn't mean you have to float along in life without a plan. It means that when you do make plans, they come from a place of appreciation and acceptance of what you currently have. In fact, mindfulness is a great tool for setting goals.

Waters advises that mindful planning involves taking a close look at what you want to be, not just what you want to have. Asking questions like, "What is my place in the world?" and "What kind of relationships do I want to cultivate?" require more self-reflection than listing things you want to buy or the size of home you'd like to have.

The following exercise will help steer you in the right direction.

Mindfulness Exercise: Mindful Goal-Setting

The next time you set a goal, ask yourself the following questions:

1. **Does this goal support my higher values?**

    When your goals support your beliefs and wider vision, you are much more likely to stick with them. Working towards a value-driven goal will also be more satisfying. For instance, setting a weight loss goal because you value health makes sense. However, setting goals just for the sake of impressing others probably won't offer much intrinsic satisfaction.

2. **Am I being realistic?**

    Set goals that stretch you, not goals that leave you feeling overwhelmed before you even begin. Be honest with yourself. Remember that goals need to be right for you, not someone else or an imaginary version of yourself.

3. **How will chasing this goal affect other people in my life?**

   You probably don't live in a vacuum, and your goals could have a direct effect on your family, friends, and colleagues. You don't have to design your life around other people, but it's sensible to think mindfully about the broader effects of your goals. You may need to adjust your goals slightly, or tweak your plans.

4. **When I imagine achieving this goal, how does my body feel?**

   Close your eyes and visualize the moment you achieve your goal. Tune into your body. How do you feel? Perhaps your heart rate has increased? Maybe you feel a rush of energy flowing through your body? Or do you find yourself sitting up straighter, in a more confident pose? These are all good signs that your goal is a great fit.

5. **Am I willing to sit with the discomfort that will come with pursuing this goal?**

   Chasing a meaningful goal will sometimes make you anxious. This is perfectly normal. As you now know, mindfulness practices will help you weather these emotions, accept them, and move forward.

However, you need to be prepared to embrace your feelings, whatever they may be, at all stages of the journey.

6. **Can I hold this goal lightly?**
As we saw in Chapter 10, clinging to a set of expectations is a recipe for disaster. Can you accept that you need to hold your goal lightly? Do you accept that your circumstances may change? As you'll see in the next section, it's good to take a flexible approach.

When You Start Living Mindfully, Your Goals Might Change

Living moment to moment and finding peace and joy in everyday activities may change you on a profound level. Too many of us mindlessly go along with the goals society has set for us. We are told that wealth, good looks, status, and fame will make us happy. We are told to go to college, work hard, get a high-powered job, and buy as many toys and status symbols as possible.

However, when you make mindfulness a part of your life, you'll probably start questioning these values. For example, you might decide that time spent in mindful relaxation with your family is more valuable than working long hours to land your next big promotion. Your old goals may no longer fit your personal aims and values. It's OK to change your goals. Review them whenever your intuition tells you it's time.

MINDFULNESS IMPROVES DECISION-MAKING

Have you ever felt torn between two or more options? Are you overwhelmed whenever you need to make a big decision? Great news: mindfulness can help you out.

Not only can mindfulness be successfully combined with decision-making, but it can improve your ability to make sensible choices.

Mindfulness Exercise: Decision-Making

Here's how to make a mindful choice:[59]

1. Be aware that you need to make the best possible decision, not a perfect decision. Acknowledge that you are in a state of confusion. Take a few deep breaths. Reassure yourself that you can only do your best with the information and resources you have available to you right now.

2. Tune into your goals and values. When decision-making is tough, it's often because two or more of your values are colliding.

    For instance, suppose you have to choose whether to walk away from your job at a small, family-run firm. On one hand, you may value loyalty and stability, which makes you reluctant to leave. At the same time, you might also value creative expression and ambition, which makes you want to seek a different kind of work.

The best decisions support as many of your values as possible, but sometimes there seems to be no winning. Reframe the situation as a chance to learn and grow. You may have to acknowledge that one of your values has to take on greater importance relative to others.

3. Weigh each option carefully. Notice whether you tend to place more weight on emotional factors than intellectual factors, or vice versa. Mindfully encourage yourself to address the problem from both sides.

4. Ask, "What might I be missing here?" and "Is there anything I'm forgetting about?" Be patient with yourself.

You'll notice a degree of discomfort when you have to make a decision, and it's this feeling that means we tend to delay them as long as possible. When we make a choice, we're giving up a sense of control. When we rule out one or more options, we are limiting our opportunities.

We often worry about making the wrong decision. We get carried away, dreaming up all kinds of scenarios in which we come to regret our choices. Mindfulness helps you accept this discomfort, which empowers you to make more decisions in the future. You'll learn to trust yourself and how to accept the outcome of your choices.

Summary

- You can learn how to balance mindfulness with long-term planning and decision-making.
- Mindful goals align with our deepest values.
- Leading a more mindful life often prompts us to re-evaluate our goals.
- Mindful decision-making entails taking a realistic look at all our options, weighing up the practical and emotional dimensions of each, and making the best decision based on the resources we have.

CHAPTER 12:

MINDFULNESS & RELATIONSHIPS

Relationships can be hard work. The good news is that adopting a more mindful way of life can strengthen your relationships, help you resolve arguments, and generally feel happier around other people.

In this chapter, we'll focus on romantic relationships, but the principles and exercises apply to friendships, family relationships, and even work relationships.

WHAT DOES A MINDFUL RELATIONSHIP LOOK LIKE?

At the beginning of your relationship, you were probably mindful of one another. You were on your best behavior. You tried to impress them with your kindness, humor, and devotion. Your priority was to keep them happy, hoping that they would stick around. When you were apart, you probably thought about them all the time.

Unfortunately, once we've settled into a relationship, we often start taking our partners for granted. Other concerns, such as work or starting a family, start to take up more of our attention.

No honeymoon period lasts forever, but you can keep your relationship intimate and fresh by making a commitment to loving your partner in a mindful way. So, what does this mean?

A mindful relationship looks like this:

- Both parties feel respected.
- Both parties feel as though their partner truly listens to them.
- Both parties know that their partner is interested in them as a person.
- Both parties know that their partner finds them attractive.
- Disagreements are handled sensitively but directly.
- Both parties understand that relationships require ongoing maintenance if they are to succeed.

Sounds good, doesn't it? Mindful relationships aren't perfect, but they are far more satisfying than sliding into the kind of rut that many of us know all too well.

COMMUNICATION: THE KEY TO SUCCESSFUL RELATIONSHIPS

Poor communication causes resentment and misunderstandings, which can ultimately ruin a relationship. All too often, we don't bother to check that we've understood what someone else is saying. Or, even worse, we don't listen properly in the first place.

For instance, are you guilty of using your phone or reading a magazine when a partner or friend is trying to talk to you? If so, you're putting your relationship in jeopardy. Your loved one probably feels disrespected and resentful, which isn't a good basis for love or friendship.

How To Be A Great Listener

When was the last time you spoke to someone who really listened to what you had to say? Someone who gave you their full attention, listened mindfully, and never interrupted? These folks are rare – and popular! They tend to have lots of friends, and they enjoy satisfying relationships. Imagine how much better your own relationships will be when you start interacting mindfully with others.

Mindfulness Exercise: Mindful Listening

1. When someone tries to start a conversation, you need to make a decision: Can you give them the attention they need and deserve, or would it be better to delay the conversation? If it's the latter, ask if you can talk later. Explain that you want to really listen to what they have to say, and you'd rather not multitask.

2. When it's time to have the conversation, stop whatever you're doing and pay attention.

3. Maintain eye contact.

4. Try not to think about what you're going to say next. Wait until the other person has finished speaking before thinking of a response. Often, we

fall into the trap of becoming distracted by our own thoughts or judgments. This prevents us from appreciating what someone is trying to tell us.

5. Hold back when it comes to giving advice. If someone asks for your opinion, then give it, but be aware that they might just want a chance to vent.

6. Try to maintain an attitude of compassionate curiosity. Until you have evidence to the contrary, assume that the other person is acting with positive intent.

Listening is a key skill for mindful arguing. As you know, mindfulness helps develop impulse control and patience, which could make all the difference to the outcome of a fight.

During tense conversations, pause – if only for two or three seconds – before responding to a provocative statement or question. Be kind to yourself. Acknowledge that you are in a tough spot and recognize any anxiety or anger that comes up. Rehearse answers in your head before speaking aloud. It's far better to take your time than say something you'll later regret. If you feel overwhelmed, excuse yourself for a couple of minutes to think through your options.

Judgments

Do you judge others? You're in good company. Almost everyone does it; it's just human nature. We also tend to jump to conclusions about someone else's behavior, even when we don't have much evidence to support our beliefs.

For example, you may notice that your partner has left some crumbs on the kitchen table, and you automatically say to yourself, "They're so messy and lazy." Or maybe they have been late home twice this week so you jump to the conclusion that they must be having an affair or that they want to avoid spending time with you.

When we start passing judgment on everyone else's behaviors, we get into trouble. We get so caught up in reacting to what they've said or done – or what we think they've done or said – that we start acting irrationally.

We don't have to get swept up in our judgments. Instead, we can choose to be mindful when they pop up. No matter how compelling your emotions, try not to assume that they are a true reflection of reality. When you find yourself angry or upset at someone else, take a few deep breaths and pay attention to what you are actually thinking and feeling. Notice each judgment. Imagine it as a bubble floating away on a breeze, or as a leaf in a stream flowing past you.

This takes practice. Judging others, whether or not we admit it, can feel good. Self-righteousness can give us a kind of energy, and even boost our self-esteem. You'll never get rid of your impulse to judge people, but you can definitely use mindfulness to limit its effect on your relationships.

Are You Hoping That Someone Else Will Change?

If you've been embarking on a period of personal growth, you've probably felt frustrated and baffled by your own behavior. Mindfulness will help you grow as a person and get more enjoyment out of life, but it isn't easy. It takes time to learn new skills, and mindfulness is no exception.

Given that we have enough trouble understanding and changing ourselves, it's foolish to expect someone else to change on demand. Everyone evolves on their own schedule, and some people never seem to grow much, if at all. To put it bluntly, someone else's path is none of your business, even if that "someone" happens to be your partner or relative.

So, if you think you'll be happy when your partner becomes more patient, or your parents become more understanding, it's time to adjust your expectations. Stop wasting your precious time and energy. Work on accepting them as they are. Your relationships will improve because you won't feel so resentful. You'll also feel free to walk away from relationships that hold you back.

Loving-Kindness Meditation, which involves sending warmth and love to someone else, helps you accept and appreciate others. Refer back to Chapter Three if you need a refresher. Practice for a few minutes every day when your relationship is going through a rough patch.

It also helps to see the other person as a teacher. When someone can't (or won't) live up to your expectations, they are teaching you a valuable lesson about accepting life as it is, not as you want it to be. When you decide to honor who someone truly is, you'll both feel better!

Paradoxically, when you decide to show someone compassion and acceptance, they are more likely to change. If you've been practicing mindfulness, you'll already have seen this phenomenon in your own life. You've probably noticed that since you started coming face to face with your thoughts and emotions and detaching yourself from self-judgment, your life is starting to take a more positive course.

Mindfulness Doesn't Make You A Human Doormat

Mindfulness helps us accept other people's annoying behaviors and makes it easier to show them compassion. You may worry that you'll end up going too far and making too many allowances for poor or abusive behavior.

However, being mindful isn't the same as being a pushover or doormat. In fact, mindfulness helps you assert your rights and pick up on signs of abuse quickly.

When you are in tune with your emotions and don't try to write them off or make excuses for others, you'll find it easier to maintain a realistic view of your relationships. Staying in the present moment lets you monitor events as they unfold. You can take a more objective stance, and decide exactly how the other person is making you feel. You will choose partners and friends on the basis of who they really are, not who you want them to be.

Summary

- A mindful relationship is built on trust, respect, and a realistic view of the other person's strengths and weaknesses.

- Mindful communication, including mindful listening, will strengthen any partnership.
- Arguments are inevitable, but approaching them mindfully makes a big difference.
- Your relationship will improve if you accept your partner for who they are and release unrealistic ideas of who you want them to be.

CHAPTER 13:

MAKING MINDFULNESS PART OF EVERYDAY LIFE

Modern life is hectic, so how can the average person make time for mindfulness practices? In this chapter, we'll take a look at how you can weave mindfulness into your everyday routine.

What Does A Mindful Day Look Like?

Don't try to do everything on this list because you'll soon get overwhelmed. Instead, pick one or two of the habits listed below and try to do them consistently for at least three weeks. You can then add another daily practice if you like. There is no single path to mindfulness; you need to find what works best for you.

Mindful Mornings

1. **Greet the day with mindfulness.**
   When you open your eyes, resist the urge to reach for your phone. Instead, take a minute to notice how you feel. What expectations do you have for

the day ahead? Do you feel tired or well-rested? Having acknowledged your feelings, slowly get out of bed. If you don't want to get up, try not to argue with yourself – just focus on the sensation of moving your body.

2. **Make your bed.**
Making your bed is a good morning ritual. It's an easy task that sets you up for the day. Plus, it's always nicer to climb into a well-made bed in the evening.

3. **Have a mindful drink of water.**
Pay attention to the feel of the glass in your hand. Notice any water droplets or condensation and whether the glass catches the light coming in through the window. As you drink the water, feel it moving from your mouth to your stomach.

4. **Greet your partner, pets, roommates, or children in a kind and mindful manner.**
Do you snap or grunt at others in the morning? Try greeting them as though you may never see them again. Take a moment to feel grateful that they are in your life.

DURING THE DAY

1. **Spend time in a natural setting.**
Ten minutes in a park or garden will restore your mental equilibrium, which in turn will make you

more mindful. If you can't get outside, at least stand or sit by the window for a few minutes.

2. **Give yourself a mindful smile.**

    How often do you take a moment to appreciate what you see in the mirror? Lots of us look at our reflections when we shave or put on makeup, but we don't often slow down and take a moment to appreciate ourselves. If we do slow down long enough to take a good look, our inner critic usually kicks in, telling us that we are too fat, too ugly, too old, and so forth.

    If you need to ground yourself, find a quiet place and look at your own face in a mirror. Look at it as though for the first time, taking in the colors, lines, and contours. If any harsh thoughts come up, label them as such and let them go. When you're ready, give yourself a smile. Feel the love and light radiate from your face.

3. **Let yourself laugh.**

    Laughing is a form of mindfulness. When you laugh, you are grounded in the present. Find a few funny video clips to enjoy, reflect on a fond memory, or share a joke with someone else.

4. **Eat and drink mindfully.**

    You might not be able to do this with every meal or snack, but try to have at least one mindful meal per day. Refer back to Chapter Two for more tips on how to eat mindfully. When you make a cup of tea or coffee, pay attention to the process. Notice the water bubbling as it reaches boiling point. Notice the color of your drink, the steam, and how the cup or mug feels in your hands. Savor the taste.

5. **Use tech mindfully**

    Refer back to Chapter Nine for tips on how to unchain yourself from your devices.

6. **Use mindfulness practices to overcome procrastination.**

    Chapter Nine contains lots of useful exercises that will help you remain calm in the face of a long to-do list.

7. **Embrace waiting as a chance to practice.**

    Next time you are stuck in traffic or waiting in a long line, use the time to put away your phone, take a few deep breaths, and notice what is going on around you. Acknowledge that you are frustrated or bored, and the waiting will probably seem more bearable.

Easing The Transition From Work To Home

1. **End your day on a mindful note**

    Before you leave work, congratulate yourself for completing your tasks. Even if your colleagues or boss don't appreciate your efforts, you can give yourself some well-earned praise. Show yourself some appreciation.

2. Use a mindfulness ritual to help you switch off from work

Develop a mindfulness practice that you use only at the end of the day. For example, if you work in an office, you could make a habit of slowly walking down the hallway when you leave, feeling your feet against the floor.

3. Be a mindful commuter

Commuting is a perfect opportunity to practice mindfulness. Pay attention to the temperature of your car, train, or bus, the view from your window, and how it feels to sit in your seat. If you use public transportation or walk to and from work, why not listen to a guided meditation?

MINDFULNESS IN THE EVENING

1. Carry out your chores mindfully

Washing the dishes, cleaning the bathroom, doing the laundry – most chores are a wonderful opportunity to practice using your senses in a mindful way. For example, if you are doing the laundry, focus on how the fabric feels against your skin, the scent of the detergent when you remove it from the machine, or the gentle noise of the tumble dryer. As you fold the clothes, take a moment to appreciate the fact you have garments to keep you warm (or cool, depending on your climate!), and that you have the equipment to keep them clean.

2. **Take a mindful shower**

   As you step into the shower, notice how the air feels against your skin. Is it cool or warm? Turn on the shower and let the water hit your skin. Adjust the temperature up and down. Turn around slowly and notice how the water feels against different parts of your body. Are some parts more sensitive than others?

   When you squeeze shower gel or shampoo from the bottle, notice its texture, temperature, and scent. Is it strong or subtle? Fresh or musky? Does it foam? If you use a loofah or sponge, rub it gently against your skin for a minute, then use firmer strokes. Notice the change in sensation.

3. **Review your day**

   Just before you go to bed, look back over your day and think about when you were most mindful. Review the mindfulness practices you used. Which worked best for you? If you didn't manage to be mindful, that's OK. No one is perfect, and you can always try again tomorrow.

4. **Practice gratitude before you go to sleep**

   Give thanks for all the good things that happened to you during the day. Even if everything seemed to go wrong, you can still be grateful for the basics. Never take things like access to clean water, shelter, and food for granted. Some people prefer to practice gratitude in the morning to set them up for the day ahead.

Be Prepared

You've probably heard the saying, "Fail to prepare, and you prepare to fail." This applies when working with habits. Take a moment to think about the barriers you might face. For instance, let's say you want to start every day with a five-minute gratitude practice.

Perhaps you're worried about drifting off to sleep and being late for work as a result. Or maybe you just have a feeling that you won't feel like spending time practicing mindfulness in the morning and would prefer to jump straight in the shower instead as usual.

With a little initiative, both of these barriers can be overcome. For example, you could make it a habit to sit up on the edge of your bed as soon as you wake up or decide to do your gratitude practice in the shower instead. You could write a note to yourself and keep it on your bedside table to read on those mornings when the last thing you want to do is set aside five minutes to be mindful.

Get An Accountability Buddy

Do you know someone else who is interested in mindfulness and personal development? If so, why not suggest you support one another on your mindfulness journeys? Checking in with a quick phone call or text message a few times per week can keep you both on track. If you don't know anyone who might be suitable, look for a buddy online. There are lots of communities, such as freemindfulness.org, where you can meet like-minded people.

Taking Your Practice Further

If you have time, set aside longer periods – say 20 to 30 minutes per day – for an extended period of practice. You could get up earlier in the morning or start your bedtime routine a half hour earlier than usual. You could even find a quiet room during your lunch break at work to meditate or engage in another mindful practice.

When you make an appointment with yourself, honor it, just as you would a meeting with a friend or coworker. If you feel a sense of resistance to scheduling time for yourself, take a moment and think about why this might be. Can you feel the resistance in your body? Does the thought of taking time for yourself feel somehow "wrong" or selfish?

If so, gently remind yourself of the benefits of mindfulness. Take an attitude of self-compassion. Caring for yourself, especially in a world that demands we put others' needs before our own, can be scary. Yet prioritizing your wellbeing can actually help those around you. For example, if you are a parent, living a more mindful life will help you remain calm when your kids are testing your patience. Your children are also more likely to develop emotional intelligence if they have parents who model healthy behaviors.

Summary

- To get the most from mindfulness practice, you need to make it a part of your everyday life.
- You can practice mindfulness at any time of day. Mundane tasks and chores often provide the perfect opportunity to engage all your senses and ground yourself in the present moment.
- Anticipate barriers to your practice and think of ways around them.
- An accountability buddy will help keep you on track.
- If you have time, aim for 20-30 minutes of practice per day.
- You are only human. Don't worry if you fall back into old habits occasionally.

CONCLUSION

Congratulations! You've discovered how to live in the present. The daily grind is no longer quite so joyless now that you can find contentment in every moment. Your relationships will blossom as others feel drawn to your positive energy. You'll find new meaning in your career, hobbies, and friendships.

The more time you make for your mindfulness practices, the lighter and freer you will become. When you feel yourself slipping into mindless behavior, you will pull yourself back to reality within seconds.

Your family, friends, and colleagues will soon notice the shift in your outlook. You'll get compliments like:

"You seem so content lately."

"You're looking so relaxed!"

"Wow, I wish I could be as calm as you."

They will start asking for your "secret." Point them in the direction of this book and encourage them to experience the power of mindfulness for themselves. Offer to share a few of your favorite practices. Why not suggest a mindful walk or meal together?

Mindfulness has the power to heal the world. If we all took time to notice and accept our emotions instead of acting on impulse and then judging ourselves, imagine how things would change. Everyone would be kinder. Relationships would be easier. Old grudges would be forgotten.

Society is gradually waking up. More than ever, we need to live consciously, accept our differences, and join together to shape our collective future. You are now part of this movement. Isn't that exciting?

You may only be one person, but your actions have a ripple effect. Treating yourself and others with quiet appreciation and respect softens your attitude to life. You will start seeing opportunity and blessings wherever you look. Sure, you'll come up against challenges, but you can handle them.

From now on, your mindfulness practice is your refuge, open at all hours of the day and night. Whatever happens, you'll always be able to surf even the biggest of waves. Embrace change, show compassion to yourself and others, and treasure this moment. Ultimately, it's all any of us have.

THANKS FOR READING!

I really hope you enjoyed this book, and most of all – got more value from it than you had to give.

It would mean a lot to me if you left an Amazon review – I will reply to all questions asked!

Simply find this book on Amazon, scroll to the reviews section, and click "Write a customer review".

Or alternatively please visit www.pristinepublish.com/mindfulnessreview to leave a review.

Be sure to check out my email list, where I am constantly adding tons of value.

The best way to currently get on it is by visiting www.pristinepublish.com/meditationbonus and entering your email.

Here I'll provide actionable information that aims to improve your enjoyment of life.

I'll update you on my latest books and I'll even send free e-books that I think you'll find useful.

Kindest regards,

Olivia Telford

Also by
Olivia Telford

With Hygge and Minimalism you will discover something that offers relaxation, happiness, and contentment, all rolled into one. They encompass the positivity and enjoyment that one can get from simple everyday things.

Visit: www.pristinepublish.com/olivia

REFERENCES

[1] Mindful Magazine. (2014). *What is Mindfulness?*

[2] Shapiro, S.L., Carlson, L.E., Astin, J.A., & Freedman, B. (2006). Mechanisms of Mindfulness. *Journal of Clinical Psychology.*

[3] Tricycle. (2017). *The Mindfulness of the Buddha.*

[4] Thera, S. (1998). *The Way of Mindfulness: The Satipatthana Sutta and Its Commentary.*

[5] O'Brien, B. (2017). *The Four Foundations of Mindfulness.*

[6] Center for Mindfulness. (n.d.). *MBSR: Mindfulness-Based Stress Reduction.*

[7] Condon, P., Desbordes, G., Miller, W.B., & DeSteno, D. (2013). Meditation Increases Compassionate Responses to Suffering. Psychological Science.

[8] de Vibe, M, et al. (2013). Mindfulness training for stress management: a randomised controlled study of medical and psychology students. BMC Medical Education.

[9] Wachs, K., & Cordova, J.V. (2007). Mindful Relating: Exploring Mindfulness & Emotion Repertoire in Intimate Relationships. *Journal of Marital and Family Therapy.*

[10] Zeidan, F., Johnson, S.K., Diamond, B.J., David, Z., & Goolkasian, P. (2010). Mindfulness meditation improves cognition: Evidence of brief mental training. Consciousness and Cognition.

[11] Black, D.S., & Slavich, G.M. (2016). Mindfulness meditation and the immune system: a systematic review of randomized control trials. Annals of the New York Academy of Science.

[12] The Tavistock & Portman NHS Foundation Trust. (n.d.). *Mindfulness: A self-help guide.*

[13] Smookler, E. (2016). *Beginner's Body Scan Meditation.*

[14] Brady, A. (n.d.). *Mindful Walking Practice: How to Get Started.*

[15] Thorpe, M. (2017). *12 Science-Based Benefits of Meditation.*

[16] Dienstmann, G. (n.d.). *Mantra Meditation – The Why, the How, and the Methods.*

[17] Koreyva, W. (n.d.). *Learn to Meditate in 6 Easy Steps.*

[18] Greater Good in Action. (n.d.). *Loving-Kindness Meditation.*

[19] Science Daily. (2017). *Yoga, Meditation improve brain function and energy levels, study shows.*

[20] Konkel, L. (n.d.). *Cortisol: Everything You Need to Know About the "Stress Hormone."*

[21] Brand, S., Holsboer-Trachsler, E., Naranjo, J.R., & Schmidt, S. (2012). Influence of Mindfulness Practice on Cortisol and Sleep in Long-Term and Short-Term Meditators. Neuropsychobiology.

[22] Positive Psychology Program. (2017). *MBSR: 25 Mindfulness-Based Stress Reduction Exercises and Courses.*

[23] Luken, M., & Sammons, A. (2016). Systematic Review of Mindfulness Practice for Reducing Job Burnout. American Journal of Occupational Therapy.

[24] O'Brien, M. (n.d.). *How to Use Mindfulness to Work with Negative Emotions.*

[25] Abblett, M. (2017). *How Labels Help: Tame Reactive Emotions by Naming Them.*

[26] Buggy, P. (n.d.). *6 Mindful Strategies for Dealing with Negativity.*

[27] Domet, S. (2018). *A Simple Mindful Gratitude Exercise.*

[28] Van Oyen Witvliet, C., Richie, F.J., & Root Luna, L.M., & Van Tongeren, D.R. (2018). Gratitude predicts hope and happiness: A two-study assessment of traits and states. *The Journal of Positive Psychology.*

[29] Schutte, N.S., & Malouff, J.M. (2011). Emotional intelligence mediates the relationship between mindfulness and subjective well-being. *Personality and Individual Differences.*

[30] Ibid.

[31] Dansiger, S. (2016). *Mindfulness for Anger Management: Transformative Skills for Overcoming Anger and Managing Powerful Emotions.* Emeryville, CA: Althea Press.

[32] Dummies. (n.d.). *How to Use Mindfulness to Cope with Anger.*

[33] NHS. (n.d.). *Symptoms: Clinical Depression.*

[34] NHS. (2019). *Mindfulness.*

[35] Beck Institute for Cognitive Behavioral Therapy. (n.d.) *History of Cognitive Behavioral Therapy.*

[36] Morrison, A.B., Goolsarran, M., Rogers, S.L., & Jha, A.J. (2014). Taming a wandering attention: Short-form mindfulness training in student cohorts. Frontiers in Human Neuroscience.

[37] Positive Psychology Program. (2018). *Gratitude Meditation: A Simple but Powerful Happiness Intervention.*

[38] Positive Psychology Program. (2017). *22 Mindfulness Exercises, Techniques & Activities for Adults.*

[39] Chiesa, A., & Serretti, A. (2011). Mindfulness based cognitive therapy for psychiatric disorders: A systematic review and meta-analysis. *Psychiatry Research.*

[40] Positive Psychology Program. (2019). *What is MBCT?*

[41] Hofmann, S.G., & Gomez, A.F. (2017). Mindfulness-Based Interventions for Anxiety and Depression. Psychiatric Clinics of North America.

[42] Abblett, M., & D'Antuono, J. (2016). *Why It's Difficult to Meditate with Anxiety.*

[43] Aryaloka Buddhist Center. (n.d.) *Mandalas as a spiritual practice.*

[44] Goldstein, E. (2013). *STOP.*

[45] National Institute for the Clinical Application of Behavioral Medicine. (n.d.). *A Simple Mindfulness Practice That Can Lower Anxiety.*

[46] Byrne, H. (2016). *The Here-and-New Habit: How Mindfulness Can Help You Break Unhealthy Habits Once and for All.* Oakland, CA: New Harbinger Publications.

[47] Kahneman, D. (2012). *Thinking, Fast and Slow.* London, England: Penguin Books Ltd.

[48] Brewer, J. (2017). *A Simple Way to Break a Bad Habit.*

[49] Clear, J. (n.d.). *How Long Does It Actually Take to Form A New Habit? (Backed By Science).*

[50] Portland Psychotherapy. (n.d). *Riding the Wave: Using Mindfulness to Help Cope with Urges.*

[51] Tice, D.M., & Baumeister, R.F. (1997). Longitudinal Study of Procrastination, Performance, Stress, and Health: The Costs & Benefits of Dawdling. *Psychological Science.*

[52] Sirois, F.M., & Tosti, N. (2012). Lost in the moment? An Investigation of Procrastination, Mindfulness, & Well-being. *Journal of Rational-Emotional and Cognitive-Behavior Therapy.*

[53] Buser, T., & Peter, N. (2012). Multitasking. Experimental Economics.

[54] Ophir, E., Nass, C., & Wagner, A.D. (2009). Cognitive control in media multitaskers. PNAS.

[55] Kubu, C., & Machado, A. (2017). *The Science is Clear: Why Multitasking Doesn't Work.*

[56] Baker, Z.G., LeRoy, A., & Krieger, H. (2016). Fear of missing out: Relationships with depression, mindfulness, and physical symptoms. *Translational Issues in Psychological Science.*

[57] Rampton, J. (2017). *7 Reasons Why Spending Money on Experiences Makes Us Happier Than Buying Stuff.*

[58] Waters, B. (2011). *The Paradox of Mindfulness and Future Planning.*

[59] Maidenberg, M. (2015). *6 Tips for Making BEST Mindful Decisions.*

Printed in Great Britain
by Amazon